NOTHING

—IS—

IMPOSSIBLE

—WITH—

GOD

JOHN MICHAEL TALBOT

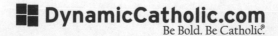

DynamicCatholic.com

Be Bold. Be Catholic.®

NOTHING IS IMPOSSIBLE WITH GOD

First Edition
Copyright © 2013 John Michael Talbot
Published by BEACON PUBLISHING

ISBN Soft Cover: 978-1-937509-61-3

The Best Version of Yourself® and
Dynamic Catholic® and Be Bold. Be Catholic.®
are registered trademarks of The Dynamic Catholic Institute.

Design by Shawna Powell

For more information on this title and
other books and CDs available through the
Dynamic Catholic Book Program, please visit:

www.DynamicCatholic.com

Printed in the United States of America.

TABLE OF CONTENTS

Part I: Testimony and Witness and the New Evangelization

Part II: Personal Prayer and Private Devotion

Part III: Walk Through the Liturgy

INTRODUCTION

We live in a troubled time. We see it in our world and in the Church. Many things simply seem impossible to fix with human effort alone. But we also face a world with exciting possibilities in God. Nothing is impossible with God.

Scripture assures us of this. During the Annunciation Gabriel tells Mary:

> And the angel answered her, "The Holy Spirit will come upon you, and the power of the Most High will overshadow you; therefore the child to be born will be called holy—the Son of God. And behold, your relative Elizabeth in her old age has also conceived a son, and this is the sixth month with her who was called barren. For nothing will be impossible with God." And Mary said, "Behold, I am the servant of the Lord; let it be to me according to your word." (Lk 1:35–38)

When Jesus is speaking to the rich young ruler who cannot renounce everything to follow him, he says, "'What is impossible with man is possible with God.' And Peter said, 'See, we have left our homes and followed you.' And he said to them, 'Truly, I say to you, there is no one who has left house or wife or brothers or parents or children, for the sake of the kingdom of God, who will not receive many times more in this time, and in the age to come eternal life.'" (Mt 19:28–30)

And finally, when speaking about the gift of faith enough to cast out demons, heal the sick, and bring conversion, Jesus says, "I say to you, if you have faith like a grain of mustard seed, you will say to this mountain, 'Move from here to there,' and it will move, and nothing will be impossible for you." (Mt 17:20)

The common problems that face us are well known. We hear about them in the news every day. Economic troubles plague a Western world that has turned from God. Political polarization is dividing once-united peoples and nations. The United States government is in gridlock. Religious freedom is being threatened even in the U.S., which was built on protecting that freedom. The most basic right to life is threatened with abortion being extended even to the last weeks of pregnancy. Some have said that we have slipped into a new barbarism. I agree. In the Church sex scandals continue to rock us, even with the election of a new pope. This new pope must be a man of great Spirit-given faith and he is certainly proving to be so! In fact, he seems so far to be the leader we need to usher in a new breath of fresh air in God's Spirit within the Church at this moment in time.

But for most of us, while these larger common problems underlie our sense of peace and security, it is the ordinary stuff of life that seems impossible. Beyond the struggle to hold down a job, make ends meet, pay off our bills, get medical care for our kids, and get them through school, unhealthy relationship patterns in the family, at work, or even at church often seem impossible to overcome. There's always that one person we just can't seem to get along with, no matter how hard we try. Then that sends us into thought and emotional patterns that are unhealthy and unsatisfying. It often seems impossible to overcome bad use of good emotions like anger, or to avoid falling into negative thoughts. But it is not. Jesus Christ and the gospel teaching of the Catholic Church have solutions to these problems. Nothing is impossible with God.

But we must admit that we are not always living our own faith very well. The Dynamic Catholic Institute says that only seventeen percent of Catholics in America attend church. Only fifteen percent of Catholic youth attend Mass on Sunday. If they were a denomination, nonpracticing Catholics would be the second-largest in America. There are now thirty million of them. And if we look to the non-Catholic megachurches down the street, fifty percent of their members are nonpracticing Catholics. They not only go to these other faith communities and churches, but they cannot wait to get there, and they don't want to leave when church is over.

This rankles some Catholics. Some criticize megachurches. There is a standard litany of reasons: They are too entertainment oriented, they don't have the Eucharist, and so on. But these are defense mechanisms at best. While I certainly do not advocate abandoning what makes our Catholic heritage so rich and wonderful, I do believe that we can learn from the success of our non-Catholic brothers and sisters. In fact, what they are now doing very well, we once did even better. We must rediscover our own Catholic heritage, and put it back into practice.

It is not about blaming them for "stealing" our people or finding fault with their theology or worship styles. It is not about theological differences. It is about seeing lively faith communities, preaching, and worship. They are not stealing our sheep. They are only doing what they do, and doing it very well. We need to begin examining why people are leaving the Catholic faith, and start doing what we do even better. Simply showing up and mumbling our way through Mass is not enough. We must become full and active participants through a lively personal faith in Christ that brings our local parish community to life again.

An often-overlooked fact of liturgical history is that St. John Chrysostom developed his liturgy at the Hagia Sophia cathedral in Constantinople to combat the heresy of Arianism and the sports events of his day, the popular Roman Circus. Arians had taken to the streets with glorious singing of hymns and celebration to win the people of the city, and it worked. Chrysostom developed one of the greatest liturgies of the Christian East, still the most widely used today, by taking the Orthodox Catholic people to the streets with singing and celebration that was even better. And it worked. That is where the Little Entrance and the Great Entrance in the Divine Liturgy of St. John Chrysostom came from. It worked so well that they continued using this practice to compete with the pageantry of the local Roman sports events.

We need to use similar creativity and celebration today, in our own time. We need our churches to be Spirit-filled places with great participation in the Liturgies, which are so well done that folks would much rather come to Mass than go to the megachurch down the street or watch Sunday football. We would think it would be more important for our children to come to parish events than to engage in a seemingly endless array of soccer or other extracurricular activities. But it is not enough to simply have another program—we already have plenty of them, and sometimes they only further divide parishes. We must tap the power of the Spirit in our life and in our parish to unite us and help us to see seemingly impossible things happen with God.

The word impossible comes from the Greek αδυνατοσ (*adynatos*). It means "without strength." The root word, δυνατοσ (*dynatos*), is similar to another Greek word, δυναμισ (*dynamis*), which means "power." It is where we get the English word dynamite, and it is used of the power of the Holy Spirit, through whom we can do seemingly impossible things. "But you will receive power when the Holy Spirit comes upon you, and you will be my witnesses in Jerusalem, throughout Judea and Samaria, and to the ends of the earth." (Acts 1:8) When the Spirit fills us we are filled with spiritual "dynamite" that can remove many human obstacles on the sensual, emotional, and rational levels that stop the healthy flow of the water of the Spirit in every part of our life.

For many years our JMT Ministry Team has been going back and forth across America visiting parishes big and small. We are seeing the power of God at work in parish after parish, and conversion in person after person. We are renewing the Church one parish at a time, and the people of God one human heart at a time—and it is working. Catholics are ready to get excited about their faith again! We are tired of the bad news. We want to focus on the Good News of Jesus again, and have it empower our parishes.

This book shares the message we have been bringing to parishes with our ministry team. We will look at three main themes: testimony, personal prayer, and a walk through the Liturgy. They will help transform us personally and in our local parish churches. This message has been most successfully received. It is simple, but powerful. It is simply to live our Catholic Christian faith with hope, joy, and faith. We will always have human problems of Church, civil government, the workplace, family relationships, and even ourselves. But Jesus says to us, "I have told you this so that you might have peace in me. In the world you will have trouble, but take courage, I have conquered the world." (Jn 16:33) Let us always remember, nothing is impossible with God.

PART I:
Testimony and Witness and the New Evangelization

I want to begin by sharing my personal testimony with you. There is a reason I do this. We Catholics have lost the art of sharing our witness for Christ and our testimony with each other in recent decades. We need to rediscover it.

The Church has encouraged us to share our stories of faith with one another as part of the New Evangelization. Some object that this is "too Protestant," or that words are not enough.

The "too Protestant" objection is typically a defensive reaction against their success regarding music, preaching, and truly engaged attendance by congregants, in contrast to our less-than-stellar record and experience in such areas. It falls away after a few minutes of calm discussion.

Regarding words: True, words must be backed up with actions, and the bishops encourage us to preach with our entire way of life. But words can and should be used at the right time. As the popular saying commonly attributed to St. Francis goes, "Preach always, and if you must, use words."

Words should and even must be used at certain times. St. Paul says, "But how can they call on him in whom they have not believed? And how can they believe in him of whom they have not heard? And how can they hear without someone to preach?

And how can people preach unless they are sent?" (Rom 9:14–15) Jesus himself says, "And you will be led before governors and kings for my sake as a witness before them and the pagans. When they hand you over, do not worry about how you are to speak or what you are to say. You will be given at that moment what you are to say. For it will not be you who speak but the Spirit of your Father speaking through you." (Mt 10:18–20)

Likewise, words must be used at the right time and in the right way. Constant quoting of Scripture, sacred tradition, or Church teaching can be as negative as saying nothing at all. St. Paul says to the Colossians, "Let your speech always be gracious, seasoned with salt, so that you know how you should respond to each one." (Col 4:6) Some scholars believe that this also means with an uplifting dose of good humor.

Scripture says, "Always be ready to give an explanation to anyone who asks you for a reason for your hope, but do it with gentleness and reverence, keeping your conscience clear, so that, when you are maligned, those who defame your good conduct in Christ may themselves be put to shame." (1 Pt 3:15–16)

So words are important. But they must be backed up by our way of life, and they must be spoken in the right way at the right time. Knowing just how and when takes a bit of wisdom. Usually that can be found through a simple dose of common sense and courtesy. And the best way to find that is to ask yourself what you would like from someone at a particular time in your life. This is nothing less than the golden rule found in most good mainline faiths and moralities of the world. Jesus said it too: "Do to others whatever you would have them do to you. This is the law and the prophets." (Mt 7:12)

But there is something even more wonderful than simply using words correctly. We become a continuation of the

Incarnation of the Word through our entire way of life in following Jesus. We become a gospel of Jesus Christ.

St. Paul says, "You are our letter, written on our hearts, known and read by all, shown to be a letter of Christ administered by us, written not in ink but by the Spirit of the living God, not on tablets of stone but on tablets that are hearts of flesh." (2 Cor 3:2–3)

We are an epistle of the apostles, and a gospel of Jesus Christ. Our entire life is preaching, whether we like it or not. We are preaching either Jesus and God or the self-obsession of the world and the devil without God. The choice is ours. As the Acts of the Apostles says, "But you will receive power when the Holy Spirit comes upon you, and you will be my witnesses in Jerusalem, throughout Judea and Samaria, and to the ends of the earth." (Acts 8)

But this can be risky business. When we share with others there is a risk that they will reject what we say. They might even reject us as human beings. This is the risk of martyrdom.

The words *witness* and *testimony* come from the Greek μαρτυσ (*martys*) and μαρτυριον (*martyrion*). It is where we get our English word *martyr*. To give our witness of Christ and the Church is to take a chance. It is a risk. We might be accepted or rejected. Some have shed their blood for their witness of Christ. This is called the "red" martyrdom. But most of us experience the "green" martyrdom of daily sacrifices of love for Jesus and others. We take the risk of martyrdom when we speak about our faith in Jesus and life in the Church.

We Catholics, and other more moderate Christians and folks of all faiths and goodwill, have developed a distinct dislike for the proverbial Bible-thumper. You know the type. If you have a problem, they have a book, chapter, and verse. We have learned to run the other way when we see them coming.

But we are not exempt from being thought of as Bible-thumpers. We Catholics have our fair share of similar devotees. We might call them "Catechism-crushers." It is the same religious animal in different theological clothes. But the basic approach is the same. It does not build up, but tears down through an unfair dose of guilt and shame. It remains lifeless and legal. All it does in the long run is repel people from the faith.

St. Paul says to speak only when it builds up another person: "No foul language should come out of your mouths, but only such as is good for needed edification, that it may impart grace to those who hear." (Eph 4:29) The word *edify* means "to build up," like an edifice. It is οικοδομη (*oikodome*) in Greek. It is the original superdome! In all seriousness, it means "family dwelling."

What we want to do is to share our faith in Christ and life in the Church with those who might be going through a period of doubt or discouragement. It is about coming to the aid of a brother or sister in a time of crisis and saying, "You know, I went through something similar. But you can make it. Jesus helped me, and he can help you too." It is about loving support, not about condemnatory guilt. It builds up; it does not tear down.

I wrote a song called "St. Theresa's Prayer" that says, "Christ has no body now, but yours." I have the audience hold hands and realize that we both give and receive the hand of Jesus in this gesture. It reminds us to reach out to hold the hands of those who might be stumbling as we all walk the path of life in Christ. We don't heartlessly drag them through the dirt. Rather, we briefly pause, and then gently but firmly hold their hands to help them back up in Christ again.

So I want to share my testimony, give my witness, and tell my story to build you up. I also want to encourage you to share your story with others in a way that builds them up in Christ.

1: MY FAMILY HERITAGE

I was born in 1954 to a Methodist mother and Presbyterian father. Most Catholics don't have a clue as to what this means, but my Protestant brothers and sisters in Christ know exactly what I mean. It is a setup for conflict that can make a child theologically schizophrenic at times!

Presbyterians were founded by John Calvin, one of the three pillars of the Protestant Reformation. The Reformers were trying to amend some of the abuses found in Latin rite Roman Catholicism at the time. Calvin believed very strongly in the providence of God, and believed in an extreme predestination of both the saved and the damned. Methodists were founded by John and Charles Wesley around a hundred years later. Charles composed many of the hymns that we now sing even in Catholic churches, albeit with updated lyrics. Methodists believe very strongly in human free will. This sets up a seeming contradiction and division: One relies on predestination, and the other on human free will.

Because my mother was born of a long line of Methodist ministers, we were raised predominantly in the Methodist Church. But my Presbyterian father just thought that it was all predestined, so it was cool anyway!

In my missions I joke with the Presbyterians and tell them they were predestined to be at a Catholic event. And then I really get the Methodists in trouble by saying that they actually chose freely to come. We have a lot of fun in our missions.

And here is the real punch line: We Catholics believe one hundred percent in both! We believe in the predestination of those who follow Jesus, but not of those who do not, and we believe in the free will to choose between the two. Theological logic alone cannot grasp the fullness of that stance. It seems like a complete contradiction. But we Catholics have an answer for this: It's a mystery! This always gets a self-aware belly laugh from Catholics.

Indeed, the center of the Catholic Christian spirituality is sacrament, especially the sacrament of the Eucharist. Sacrament simply means "sacred mystery." (In the ancient Eastern Christian Churches they rarely speak of "sacrament," which is based on a Latin word; rather, they speak of "mystery," based on the Greek μυστηριον, or mysterion, from "to shut the mouth," meaning simply something beyond words.) This means that while there are things about our faith that we can understand and explain, there are also many things that are real and deeply true, but that cannot be fully understood or explained.

This is true because the essence of our Christian faith is God's love, and love remains a mystery. There are things that we can understand about love, and there are things that we cannot fully understand. In essence, God's love can be partly but not fully understood. This is because God is infinite. Scripture says, "What eye has not seen, and ear has not heard, and what has not entered the human heart, what God has prepared for those who love him." (1 Cor 2:9)

Yet there are things that we can definitely know about God. Especially in Jesus we can say with John:

"What was from the beginning, what we have heard, what we have seen with our eyes, what we looked upon and touched with our hands concerns the Word of life—for the life was made visible; we have seen it and testify to it and proclaim to you the eternal life that was with the Father and was made visible to us—what we have seen and heard we proclaim now to you, so that you too may have fellowship with us; for our fellowship is with the Father and with his Son, Jesus Christ." (1 Jn 1:1–3)

There are two mistakes to avoid here. First, believing love is only a feeling; and second, believing love is only an act of logic. Love is a decision and an act of the human will. But the will is neither feelings nor cold logic alone. It is a decision that includes and guides the emotions. Feelings alone rise and fall. And logic alone leaves us cold and heartless.

Theologically these two approaches can be expressed through the ideas of transcendence and immanence. He is "wholly other," beyond creation and transcendent. But he is also immanent—he can be seen in and through creation. Jesus is the ultimate emanation of God in the Incarnation, which means "in flesh," or "in red meat."

I come from a long line of Methodist preachers and evangelists on my mother's side. My grandfather, James Cochran, and my grandmother, Maggie, were a Methodist preacher and his wife who started churches all over eastern Oklahoma and western Arkansas. My grandfather would sing and draw a crowd, and then he would preach the gospel to them. Then they would start a church in a town where there were no churches yet.

When my grandmother was in her eighties I had the pleasure of spending some time with her after becoming a Catholic and beginning my current life and ministry. She had lived a wealth of American history during her lifetime, ranging from the time right after the Civil War to the moon landing, and I wanted to just hang out with her to listen to her life stories and gain some of her wisdom. We would sit together while she watched her "stories" (the soaps) on TV, and occasionally talk.

At one point she looked intently at me. I was dressed in my monastic habit. She looked me square in the eye and said, "Johnny, now that you have become a Catholic . . ." And I thought, "Oh, baby, here it comes!" She continued, "I think you're a better Methodist than ever." I smiled in great relief.

True Catholicism takes the best aspects of human ideology, philosophy, and religious belief, especially Christian ones, "baptizes" them through the waters of apostolic tradition, and brings everything together in a way that is universal and full. Jesus said, "I came so that they might have life and have it more abundantly." (Jn 10:10) The word catholic comes from the Greek καθολικός (*katholikos*), meaning "universal, full." So I had no problem thinking of myself as a Catholic "Methodist." After all, John Wesley was a genius of organizing small renewal groups in the Anglican Church in a way not unlike St. Francis in the thirteenth century. Francis said, "The world is my cloister." John Wesley said, "The world is my parish." So if Grandma wanted to call me "a better Methodist than ever," it worked for me.

Now let me tell you a joke that my saintly Methodist grandmother told me as we sat in her den in Muskogee, Oklahoma.

In the early days of the twentieth century when Grandmother and Granddad were ministering in Oklahoma, a tent revival came to their town. Back in those days Southern Baptists usually conducted the tent revivals. Pentecostalism started in America in 1904 - 1906 in Topeka, Kansas; Hot Springs, Arkansas; and

Azusa Street in Los Angeles. But it had not yet spread across the nation, so the Southern Baptists had a corner on the market of tent revivals, and this tent revival was Southern Baptist.

Since my grandmother was the wife of the town preacher, she figured that she should go check it out. They were singing, clapping their hands, stomping their feet, and raising the roof of the tent (which is not the way Catholics sing!). It was really inspirational. Then the preacher got up to speak, and he motivated people. He didn't just dispense doctrine, but motivated folks by sharing his faith. (Faith has a way of stirring up faith.) Then he called folks forward in an altar call to give their lives to Jesus, and most everyone came forward that night. Grandma liked it because Granddad was an inspirational singer who attracted crowds, preached to them, and founded churches. Finally, they gave the benediction, and then dismissed the people.

On the way out the people were aggressively shaking the pastor's hand and saying demonstrative things like, "Praise God! God moved powerfully in our midst tonight!" The pastor would answer in a similar manner. One by one, the congregation filed out in much the same way.

Then my little Methodist-minister's-wife grandma came up to him. Now, if Methodists are anything, they are polite. (Just make sure to bring a covered dish!) She gently took him by the hand and she got really excited and said, "Pastor, I want to thank you for such a lovely, lovely, lovely service. The singing was so inspirational, and the preaching was so motivational. And when you called everyone to come give their life to Jesus, I wanted to come too, but, you see, I already had."

He looked back at her and said, "Well, sister, I thank you, and I can see that you're a woman of faith. But do you mind if I ask you what church you attend?"

She said, "No, pastor, that would be fine. I'm married to the local Methodist minister, and his brothers are all Methodist ministers, and their daddy before them was a Methodist minister, and all his brothers were Methodist ministers. So, pastor, I'm a Methodist."

Now, you know what he was thinking: "You can sleep in the garage, but it doesn't make you a car." St. Augustine said pretty much the same thing when he asserted that being baptized doesn't mean that you're saved. Baptism effects grace and leaves an indelible mark on the soul signifying that the grace of God was offered. But it's up to us as to what we do with the gift. So it's really a very Catholic idea.

So the pastor continued, "Do you mind if I ask you another question?"

She said, "Not at all, pastor. We're having a wonderful interfaith dialogue!"

So the pastor kept going: "Well, sister, suppose you were married to an idiot, and all his brothers were idiots, and their daddy before them was an . . . idiot. Sister, what would that make you?"

Then my grandmother looked him square in the eye, and with all the politeness her little Methodist soul could muster, she said, "Well, pastor . . ." And she paused for the fullest possible effect and said, "That would make me a Southern Baptist." The crowd usually belly-laughs at this. But there are some uncomfortable feelings of the reality of denominational division as well.

You know, we have to learn to laugh with each other, because if we don't, all the divisions in Christianity will make us cry. Not all hard-core Baptists know this yet, but there'll be some Catholics in heaven too. And some of the new breed of ultraconservative Catholics don't know it, but there'll be some Baptists there as well. In all seriousness, St. John of the Cross said only one question will be asked of us when we stand before God: How well have you loved? Think about it—all our doctrines about God, Jesus, and our life as Church in Christ are based on the simple reality of divine love. And as Pope Francis recently said in an interview with a secular paper: "And I believe in God, not in a Catholic God, there is no Catholic God, there is God and I believe in Jesus Christ, his incarnation." This is nothing new. It is solid Catholic teaching about God and the Church.

There is plenty more to share about my family. But for now let it suffice to say that I am most grateful for a great family. Despite the human failings of every member, they provided an environment of love and security for me to grow up in. I am especially grateful for the seeds of the Christian faith that they planted in my soul from the beginning. They never forced me, but the gospel of Jesus was always there in the background. From there it was up to me to make my own faith decision. That would come. But not all at once.

2: MUSIC AND CONVERSION

Music has always been considered a most adept art form through which to express and stir up spiritual experience. The Hindus say that God created through music, and that creation is a song sung into existence by God. St. Augustine said that those who sing pray twice.

I started making music when I was eight years old. My mom and dad were musically inclined. My older brother was already a promising guitarist, and my sister was a great singer. We all sang in church, and I loved listening to my family sing. I was drawn to the guitar, but I also liked the drums. So in my young mind I thought you could put them together in the banjo.

I started playing the banjo first, and I had some really great teachers, one of whom had studied under a national champion who had played with greats like Earl Scruggs, Bill Keith, and J. D. Crowe. He passed on the best of the best to me; I was very fortunate. So by the time I was ten I was playing Bach on the five-string banjo, and I was playing professionally in a family-based folk group called the Quinchords. (We later joked that there were five of us and most of us knew roughly five chords.)

By the time I was twelve a "little" band from Britain, also known as the Beatles, had invaded America. Along with countless other folkies, my family and I traded in our acoustic instruments for electric guitars. We moved to Indiana, put together a band called the Four Score, and entered the Battle of the Bands at the Indiana state fair. We were very fortunate, for out of a couple hundred bands, we won first place that year.

For placing first we won a little record contract. I mean a really little record contract! We got to go to Chicago and record at the famous Universal Studios and cut a single. The Beatles were known around the world. But our record got circulated in about three counties! (We ended up touring in three Midwest states.)

Now, the way this worked was that we got to play places like Knights of Columbus halls and rodeo grounds at county fairs. Most of the girls wanted to go to the Coliseum at the state fairgrounds in Indianapolis to hear the Beatles, the Byrds, and the Beach Boys. When they couldn't get there, then they went to the local rodeo grounds to hear us, and they pretended we were the Beatles. But that was OK with us, because we were pretending like we were the Beatles too.

We soon teamed up with a more established local band called the Sounds Unlimited, and stretched out to a somewhat larger audience. Through a rotation of band members we grew as rock music evolved into acid and hard rock. We recorded a bit more, but were really going nowhere.

Then around 1968 the Byrds put out a record called Sweetheart of the Rodeo, which revolutionized pop music and for all intents and purposes created a new music genre called "country rock." There were a couple of bands with a similar sound at that time, but after that all kinds of new groups were birthed, including the Flying Burrito Brothers, Poco, and Great Speckled Bird, from Canada. The Eagles were the ones who finally made the genre a huge success, giving it a permanent place in American music history. Without country rock there simply would be no modern country music as we know it today.

Our producer in Chicago, Bill Trout, knew we also had a country rock background, so he suggested that we get on board. We changed the name of our band to Mason Proffit (based on Frank Proffitt, who wrote the legendary song "Tom Dooley") and went into the studio. We recorded five records and ended up on the Warner Bros. record label. We were one of those "almost famous" bands. But many higher-ups in the music industry were watching us and thought we would be the next supergroup. We brought a combination of phenomenal live performances, thanks to my older brother's charismatic stage presence, and a use of bluegrass that was relatively new at the time. Most country rock aficionados today agree that we were one of the most overlooked bands that greatly influenced the genre, and were the best band that never made it.

What this meant was that we got to play with everyone we thought we wanted to be like. We got to share stages, dressing rooms, and hotel parties with the great supergroups and stars of the era. We never played with the Beatles, the Stones, The Who, Hendrix, or Dylan, but we played with almost anyone else you can think of.

What I discovered was that the people who had everything I thought I wanted were actually still pretty unsatisfied, and some were desperately unhappy. They were good and greatly talented folks, but they were really not very happy. Some went on to take their own lives. Others sobered up and went through their own form of conversion, which often included a spiritual component. I began to wonder: What is missing? What happens after the strings stop vibrating? There had to be something more.

So I began a search. I started reading, and reading a lot. We did three hundred concerts a year, sometimes riding our converted Trailways bus twelve to eighteen hours between concerts. There were no kitchens, bedrooms, or lounges with TVs on those buses. We spent a lot of time on that bus, and we had a choice: sleep, get stoned, or read. I chose to read.

I started reading philosophy and religion. From China I read about Taoism and Confucianism. From India I read about what we call Hinduism and Buddhism. In Middle Eastern readings I concentrated on the Kabbalah, from Jewish mysticism, and Sufism, from mystical Islam. I also enjoyed reading the Greek philosophers, who spoke eloquently of the one God, and mystical language, which has stayed with us to this day in Christian mysticism. I was also reading a Revised Standard Bible, which my grandmother had given me, and those red letters were jumping out!

Somehow, Jesus said all and more of what the other great founders and teachers of the major religions and philosophies had said, but in a way that was very simple and deep. Every religion said something beautiful, and I was drawn to the mystical tradition of all of them, but Jesus seemed to say it all in a way that was both simpler and deeper than any other. I was on the road to conversion, a decision that would forever change the direction of my life, and change it for the better.

So I began to pray every day. I would come back to the hotel after a concert and pray. I also prayed all day as I read these rich spiritual sources, especially the Bible. But I got no answer. I prayed for more than a year, and still I got no answer. I was learning about God, but I did not yet know God.

I think this is important. How many of you pray but don't seem to get an answer to your prayers? I think God tests us to see if we are serious. He wants to know if we are really ready to receive his answer, not just the answer we want. God answers every prayer, but in the way and the time that is best suited for each one of us. He knows just the right time to answer far better than we do.

Finally, after I prayed for more than a year with no answer, God answered my prayer. I had an experience of Jesus that was as real as if he were sitting right next to me. Some say I had a vision of Jesus; some say it was just a psychological phenomenon. I cannot say what it was. But God created me with a psychology, so if he wants to use my psychology to reach me entirely, that is fine with me. I just knew it was real.

Jesus did not speak to me. He didn't give me a "great commission," or a vision about my life or ministry. He was simply present to me. I had asked God, "Who are you, a he, she, or it?" I didn't care what the answer was. I had no agenda, or, as we say in the South, "I have no dog in this hunt." I just wanted to know. And that question was being answered in the person of Jesus. I didn't know any theology. I hadn't yet gone back to church. All I knew was that my search for God was being answered in the person of Jesus Christ.

I also knew that I was loved, that Jesus loved me like I had not been loved before. It was not like I did not know love; I did. I grew up in a wonderful family. I was the youngest, so Mom and Dad had figured out the parenting thing by the time I was born, and I had an older brother and sister who loved me. It was an ideal childhood. I was surrounded by a warm and secure blanket of love as a child. But the love I experienced in Jesus made even the best of family love pale by comparison. Jesus loved me, and now I knew it. This was not an idea—it was an experience, and one that changed my life forever.

I also knew that my sins were forgiven. And at that point in my young life, they were starting to stack up. Do any of you sin? Of course you do. We all do. I didn't know how, but I knew Jesus had forgiven my sins, and it felt wonderful.

3: JESUS MUSIC AND CATHOLICISM

After accepting Jesus I got involved with the Jesus movement. It was called "Jesus music" before it was called "Christian con- Christian Contemporary Music" (CCM). I ended up making a record with Sparrow Records. Back then it was five artists, and fourteen employees in Canoga Park, California. It's now the biggest Christian record company in the world.

At first this transition happened when Terry, my older brother, and I began writing songs with Jesus lyrics and spiritual overtones with Mason Proffit. That attracted the attention of some Jesus freaks in the Jesus movement, who began to attend our concerts. We soon met some of the founding generation of Jesus music. My sister was hanging out with "E" Band (later Petra) and Randy Matthews. Randy would come by our family's house in Indianapolis when we visited, and share about Jesus music. We were mildly interested.

In 1972 Terry and I left the band to do a record with Warner Bros. called The Talbot Brothers. We used Bill Halverson, who'd had a good run with Crosby, Stills & Nash. It was overtly Christian, and we used the very best country rock players available. It was a great record. But Joe Smith at Warner's wanted another Mason Proffit record because, unbeknownst to me, he had slotted us to be their next major band. But we were worn out, and tired of the tensions of band life. After we recorded The Talbot Brothers, Joe was upset and decided not to promote it, so we toured the country with no record company support. We were again the greatest act that never made it.

I moved to a small farm in Indiana, and my brother took some time off. In a couple of years we put together a more Christian Mason Proffit, and tried to sell it to Clive Davis, at Arista. But he wasn't interested. So I decided to try my luck as a folk soloist. I ended up recording my first Christian album at Sparrow with Billy Ray Hearn in 1976.

As a result, I toured all across the country in every kind of church, Christian coffeehouse, and Christian college you can think of. Sometimes there were thousands there; sometimes there were more people on the stage than in the audience (and I was a soloist!). We would open the windows of a coffeehouse and turn up the PA. By the end of the night there would be hundreds there. It was a phenomenal time, at the height of the Jesus movement. They were baptizing three thousand kids a week in the Pacific Ocean in California. All we had to do was "get up on our surfboards and ride." God was truly at work in a way that was beyond mere human manipulation.

But I soon encountered troubling things. I would show up in the church in a town and I would see three things: 1) Its members were good people, 2) they had the Holy Spirit, and 3) they went to the Bible alone to figure out how to follow Jesus as a united church. I would do my ministry and we would all get along great. Then they would take me to the airport, or I would drive off to another church in another town.

The same thing would happen in this new town. Now, this is important, so follow me: They also 1) were good people, 2) were filled with the Spirit, and 3) would go to the Bible alone to figure out how to follow Jesus as a church. But then I would find out that they were divided from the church I had just visited, and they wouldn't fellowship with that church. Plus, the next time I went back to the other church I would say, "You know, those guys really don't like you guys." And they would say, "That's OK, because we really don't like them either!"

This division broke my heart. The Jesus I knew healed people; he didn't divide them. When I accepted Jesus people said, "What happened to John? He's actually a pretty nice guy!" (Remember, musicians are notoriously self-obsessed, egotistical, and just plain lazy.) Jesus made people better, not worse. It broke my heart to see folks fight about him. Something was missing. So I set out to find the missing part in my Christian experience.

I stumbled onto what I now know is called patristics, or patrology, the study of the writings of the early Church fathers. Though I was theologically unsophisticated, I was an avid reader. I knew this much: The Bible was written and compiled by the God-given authority of the early Church. So if there was a debatable passage of the Bible that was dividing us today, it just made sense to go back to the early Church to see if they had at least a substantial agreement about how to live that scripture and apply it to our situation in a developed way. That was my plan. So I began to read the fathers.

What I discovered shocked me to the core, yet attracted me irresistibly: The early Church fathers were completely Catholic! Everything that we now call "Catholic" was present in the early Church in a primitive way: apostolic succession of the bishops and a special place of leadership for the Bishop of Rome; and the sacraments, especially the Eucharist, the communion of saints living and departed, and a special devotion to Mary, the Mother of Jesus. It was not yet fully developed, but it had clearly been in place right from the beginning and through the first couple of centuries of the early Church. It was from that Church that the Scriptures were written and compiled. You needed the Church to understand them. And it is through the Scriptures that most of us learn about the life of Jesus. So we need the Church in order to receive and understand Jesus fully. The two are intrinsically linked.

Now, you need to understand, I did not want to be a Catholic. I wasn't looking to be a Catholic. I didn't even like Catholics! (I'm still working on that one, and most Catholics are too.) Like they say, if you find the perfect church, don't join it, or you'll ruin it. We look for God's perfection in the Church, not perfect pastors or members. To expect that is an exercise in frustration.

But God gave me a word: "The Catholic Church is my first Church. I love her most deeply. But she has been sick, and nearly died. I am going to raise her up to new life, and I want you to be a part of her." So in 1977 I sought out a Franciscan Catholic priest, moved into a hermitage in the woods, and placed myself under his direction. We met every day as he gave me book after book to read, until I was quietly received into the Catholic Church in an Upper Room Chapel at the now closed Alverna Franciscan Retreat Center, in Indianapolis. It was February 1978.

When I became a Catholic I went to the record company and said, "I've got good news!"

They were a gospel (Good News) music record company, so they said, "What's the good news, brother?"

I excitedly said, "I've become a . . . CATHOLIC!"

Their expressions markedly dropped as they said, "Oh . . . don't you know that you can't be a Catholic and a Christian?" (How many of us Catholics have heard that from our Evangelical and Fundamentalist friends?)

I responded, "Well, when I read about Sts. Francis and Clare, Benedict and Scholastica, Teresa of Avila and John of the Cross, and the great monastics and mystics, I am drawn closer to Jesus. I figure that if they could get radical for Christ, maybe I can too."

So they said, "Well, then we'll support you. You can make one more record."

I did. It was called The Lord's Supper, and it became the biggest record in Christian music that year. Then I released Come to the Quiet, and it sold three times more. When we let go of our agendas and plans and give them entirely to God, he will surprise us with his own plans and agendas that use our gifts, our talents, and our entire lives more successfully than we can ever do ourselves. We may not be rich or famous, but we will find personal success and a happiness we cannot find without Jesus. This is what happened to me when I became a Catholic. He is healing us, raising us up to new life, and he wants us to be a part of the Catholic Church.

I share that with you now not to make you become a Catholic, or because my testimony is so great, but because I believe we live in a time when this message of the Church being healed and raised up again is timelier than ever before in our lifetime. The sex scandals have reduced the moral authority of the Catholic Church internationally. Other secular and religious institutions have been rocked by similar sex scandals, but the Catholic Church is the largest single institution of humanitarian help and religion in the world, and we must hold ourselves to a higher standard.

There are also attacks on the Church in places where we never thought this would happen. The growing barbarism of the West has hurtled our society closer to the atrocities of ancient Rome than we have ever been before. Sexual promiscuity that reduces partners to objects of pleasure, consumerism that consumes the consumer and the poor, and a self-obsessed individualism have opened the door to widespread abortion, personal and national debt, and attacks on religious freedom we never dreamed we would face in America, much less in the rest of Western culture.

But Jesus gives us the answer if we will but receive it. As Pope Paul VI said, "Peace is possible; therefore it is a duty." The media continues to hammer away at the Catholic Church with criticism based on half-truths or outright prejudice, and we begin to believe them ourselves. You know the old saying of dictators: "Tell the people a lie long enough, and they will soon begin to believe that it is the truth." We begin to lose our joy, our hope, and even our faith.

But as I travel across the country I sense that Catholics are ready to get excited about their faith again. We are tired of the bad news. For every reason to report bad news there are millions of clergy and laity who are engaged in wonderful ministries that are reasons to celebrate the Good News of Jesus Christ.

So let's lighten up a bit. Popes come and go. We've had plenty of saints, but we've also had some scoundrels and terrible sinners as popes in our history. Bishops come and go. There've been saints and sinners. Parish priests (sorry, Father!) come and go. Some are saints, and some are sinners. Praise God! Even the local parish and pastoral council comes and goes.

But , because guess who does not come and go? Jesus! The book of Hebrews says that Jesus is the same "yesterday, today, and forever." (Heb 13:8) If we focus on Jesus, he will give us all we need to face any challenge in the Church or the world.

It is like when Jesus called Peter out of the boat to walk on water. As long as Peter focused on Jesus, he could walk in a miracle. But as soon as he took his eyes off Jesus and looked at the storm, he began to sink. The same is true with us. If we keep our eyes on Jesus we can walk in miracles! But if we take our eyes off him and look at the problems of the Church or the world, we will begin to sink into the storm waves of discouragement and depression. So focus on Jesus, and become a walking miracle for God.

The Catholic Church has been sick, and has nearly died. But Jesus is going to heal us and raise us up to new life. He wants you to be a part of her. Don't give up. Focus on Jesus, and watch the miracle unfold. Nothing is impossible with God!

PART II:
Personal Prayer and Private Devotion

Sometimes it seems that the world and even the Church are beyond reform and renewal. The darkness seems all-encompassing and suffocating. But nothing is impossible with God! Reform and renewal are possible. Reform straightens structures of the body of governments, the Church, and people. Renewal enlivens the spirit and soul of all.

Before the Church can be renewed, people must be renewed. Before the world can change, we must change. This is what personal prayer and private devotion are all about. Programs are helpful, but they cannot renew the Church. Only Jesus and the Holy Spirit can renew the Church. Programs can reform, but only the Spirit can renew. Both are needed, but the final point is renewal, not reform. Reform without renewal is dead, while renewal without reform is often fluffy and formless. We need both. The Spirit works by renewing the human heart. It is there that we must begin.

In this section we will be looking at personal prayer and devotion. Specifically we will talk about two rosaries, one from the Christian West, and one from the Christian East.

A Rosary is a repetitive prayer prayed on a knotted cord or beads. Most major religions have rosaries. In India Hindus and

Buddhists have rosaries. In the Holy Land Moslems pray the 99 Names of God on a rosary, and Eastern Orthodox and Eastern Catholics pray a Jesus Prayer Rosary. Of course, Latin rite Catholics pray the Marian Rosary in the West and throughout the world. Even some Anglicans pray a Rosary. I have heard of more and more Lutherans and Evangelicals learning to pray the Rosary in a way that truly builds up their faith in Jesus. It might be good to find your rosary and just hold it, and look at it for a moment.

Some would object and say that Jesus condemned repetitive prayer. But that is a misreading of his words, and of early Church understanding. Jesus condemned "vain" repetition, not repetition in itself.

The Greek word for "vain" is ματην (*maten*), meaning "fruitless." Something that is vain is fruitless; it bears no spiritual fruit. We find it in Jesus's condemnation of repeating religious words without really believing them.

Jesus quotes Isaiah when he says, "This people honors me with their lips, but their hearts are far from me; in vain do they worship me, teaching as doctrines human precepts." (Mt 15:8–9) If you look to the original text from the Septuagint or the Greek version quoted here, the sense is that they are using words in worship that are merely repeated with their lips and not from the heart, and they become mere human precepts.

Jesus taught the Our Father, or Lord's Prayer, in contrast to such repetition.

"In praying, do not babble like the pagans, who think that they will be heard because of their many words. Do not be like them. Your Father knows what you need before you ask him. This is how you are to pray: Our Father in heaven . . ." (Mt 6:7–9)

The early Church prayed the Lord's Prayer three times a day. Chapter 8 of The Didache, or "The Teaching of the Twelve Apostles," says:

"But let not your fasts be with the hypocrites (Mt 6:16); for they fast on the second and fifth day of the week; but fast on the fourth day and the Preparation (Friday). Neither pray as the hypocrites; but as the Lord commanded in His Gospel, thus pray: Our Father who art in heaven, hallowed be Your name. Your kingdom come. Your will be done, as in heaven, so on earth. Give us today our daily (needful) bread, and forgive us our debt as we also forgive our debtors. And bring us not into temptation, but deliver us from the evil one (or, evil); for Yours is the power and the glory for ever. Pray this three times a day."

Yet, we have often turned the repetitive praying of the Lord's Prayer into a violation of this prayer. Often we speed through such prayers. I have heard the Marian Rosary run through like the calling of a horse race, which makes it impossible to really pray, much less keep up with verbally. Imagine our voices coming through the speakers at the racetrack: "Haaiill Mary full of grace . . . and they're coming around the fourth turn!" Pretty scary, isn't it? But that is what is heard at many parishes before or after Mass.

Sometimes I feel myself out of breath during a Liturgy when trying to keep pace with the congregation. I catch every other line at best, and miss the point of the Our Father while trying to match the breakneck speed of the congregational recitation of the prayer. I cannot judge the personal faith of the individuals praying the prayer, but I can say that it is bad liturgy at best. It is using a right thing wrong.

I remember a cardinal praying Vespers with us in his cathedral teaching us this lesson. When we got to the Our Father, we prayed at the usual parish pace. He stopped us and said, "You are violating the purpose of the Lord's Prayer by the way you are praying it!" Wow! He made us slow down and pray it again like we meant it. I figure if a cardinal archbishop of the Church can do this, so can I.

So, repetition is not the issue. Vain repetition is.

WEST AND EAST

We are going to look at two rosaries, one from the Christian West, and one from the Christian East. Why?

Using Pauline language in "Ut Unum Sint, That They May Be One," May 25, 1995, Pope John Paul II said that the Church is a body, and as a body she has two lungs, an Eastern and a Western one. He said, "an expression which I have frequently employed finds its deepest meaning: The Church must breathe with her two lungs!"

Close your eyes and focus on your two lungs. Now, take a deep breath.

The word for "spirit," human and divine, in Greek is πνευμα (pneuma), and means "breath, wind, and air" of a rational creature. If we are to get the full breath of God, the Spirit, we must breathe with both lungs. As a singer I am reminded that I must be able to breathe deeply in order to sing well. My spiritual father was a Franciscan who suffered from the epidemic tuberculosis in seminaries and religious houses in the early twentieth century, and had one of his lungs removed. As much as he loved music, he could never sing like he wanted to, because he couldn't get a full breath. Likewise, in order for your spiritual life to "sing," you must breathe from both lungs, and get a full "breath" of the Spirit of God.

This does not mean that we are supposed to switch to an Eastern rite, but we are supposed to be reasonably aware of the width and breadth of the East and West of the Catholic Church. What are those rites?

The Catholic Church is made up of some twenty-two liturgical rites. Only a few of them are Western, and only one is a Latin, or Roman, rite. The Latin Rite means not that we pray the Liturgy in Latin, but that we use a vernacular translation based on the Latin translation of the original Greek and other ancient liturgical languages. Latin was the vernacular of Rome, and Greek was no longer understandable by the average person. All the others are Eastern rites, and translate the Liturgy into the vernacular directly from the original Eastern languages of Greek, Aramaic, and Coptic (early Egyptian), just to name three. The Latin rite is the largest, but it is only one, and it represents only the West.

There is a reason for this. In the early Church there were originally four, then five sees, or patriarchates, that had bishops or patriarchs of major dioceses (regions) that traced their succession back to apostolic antiquity. They were Alexandria, Antioch, Jerusalem, and Rome. After the splitting of the Roman Empire into east and west, Constantinople was added. Out of the five the Bishop of Rome held precedence, followed by the Patriarch of the New Rome in Constantinople.

Out of the five only the Roman was a Western rite. But it spread throughout Western Europe, then to the New World in the Americas, and then around the globe. Even Protestants and Anglicans are attempted reforms of the Latin Rite.

As I look across my normal mission congregation I ask which Church folks are from. Most are Roman Catholic, or from a Protestant tradition. Only a few are Eastern Catholic rite, or from an Eastern Orthodox or Oriental Church. So chances are most everyone who attends my missions is breathing only from the Western lung of the body of Christ. Let's go on now to look at both the Western and Eastern Christian rosaries, and start breathing with both lungs again!

1: THE MARIAN ROSARY

Let's begin with the Western "lung" of the body of Christ, the Church. Take a breath of the "wind" of the Spirit of God. Now breathe it out, and let go of anything in your life keeping you from the Spirit of God. Relax a bit. Now we're ready to begin with a Western Rosary.

The Rosary most recognized in the Christian West is the Marian Rosary. It is so commonly understood that we usually just call it "the Rosary," and everyone knows what it means. Or at least we think we do. But there is a history and purpose to the Rosary that we often overlook.

Many pray the Rosary daily, but fail to get the full benefit of this rich and wonderful devotion, not only because we rush through it mindlessly but also because we do not understand it fully. When we understand its history and purpose, we quite naturally begin to pray this wonderful prayer more devoutly. The history and purpose of the Rosary are related, and pretty simple. It is no deep, dark mystery, but it is often misunderstood; therefore we also miss its deeper meaning. What is that history and purpose?

MONASTIC PRAYER OF THE PSALMS

The monks of old used to pray the entire 150 Psalms daily. Since most of the monastic candidates were illiterate, part of the novitiate was to learn to read so that they could read and memorize the Psalter and most of the New Testament. This was because they did not have enough books to use for private or common prayer, so their prayers were prayed from memory. That meant that they memorized the entire Psalter and most of the New Testament in a year or so. That's a lot of Bible!

It also meant that they were turning the Scriptures in their mind most of the time. They were thinking the Scriptures literally all day. This has radical effects.

Scriptures say that we are what we think. The New King James translates Proverbs 23:7 as "For as he thinks in his heart, so is he." It is an obscure Hebrew text that translates obscurely, but the point is clear: If you fill your mind with something, it changes your heart and soul. If you think it, you become it. Perhaps that is why Psalm 1 says to "Meditate on the law of the Lord day and night." (NIV) In modern language we would say, "Garbage in, garbage out."

So as the monks of old filled their minds with the positive and wonderful things of Jesus, it changed their lives, and changed them for the better. As St. Paul said to the Romans, "Do not conform yourselves to this age but be transformed by the renewal of your mind, that you may discern what is the will of God, what is good and pleasing and perfect," (Rom 12:2) and to the Philippians, "Whatever is honorable, whatever is just, whatever is pure, whatever is lovely, whatever is gracious, if there is any excellence and if there is anything worthy of praise, think about these things." (Phil 4:8)

The lay folks who observed this wonderful change in the monks wanted to do something similar, but they could not read. So they used the simple prayers they had memorized to do something similar. They took the Our Father, the biblical section of the Hail Mary, and the Glory Be, and said them 150 times.

The Our Father taught them to pray to God as a father who loves them. The Hail Mary fully revealed that love by teaching the Incarnation of God as a man in Jesus. And the Glory Be taught that love within God is the ultimate destination of the followers of Jesus. It was really a very complete prayer method.

Some collected 150 pebbles for the 150 Psalms, and carried them in a little bag. But then the bag got heavy, and they began to lose the pebbles. So they started using cords or strings with 150 knots or beads. Well, it started to get a bit boring. So they broke the monotony by breaking the 150 into decades around the mysteries of the life of Jesus Christ, and Mary's participation in those sacred mysteries. Mary was considered a symbol, model, and mother of the faithful followers of Jesus from the earliest decades of the Church (Jn 19:26, 27; Rv 12). So, the Rosary was born.

What is important here is that the focus of the Marian Rosary is not really Mary, though we honor her as the Mother of God Incarnate in Jesus Christ. The focus of the Rosary is Jesus. What is it we Catholics have always said? "To Jesus through Mary." If we ever get stuck on Mary while praying the Rosary, we are praying the right Rosary wrong. We are not making the journey to Jesus, but this journey is always the main point of the Marian Rosary.

There is a further development in the Rosary that makes it even more wonderful. It is not a dead ritual, but a devotion that is alive, and that grows through each generation of the Church. What is that history? Let's take a brief overview.

St. Dominic popularized the devotion in the thirteenth century by preaching the 150-decade Rosary. This included much of what we know today, but with only the first part of the Ave Maria that is explicitly found in Scripture in Luke 1:28.

This was done in response to a vision that instructed him to popularize devotion to Mary as a way to lead people more fully to Jesus, whom the mendicant orders like the Dominicans and Franciscans imitated and preached so ardently.

According to Fr. Luke Wadding, one of the first Franciscan historians, in the fifteenth century a little Franciscan brother named James in Assisi had a similar vision, but his was to combine the Joyful and Glorious Mysteries into a seven-decade Rosary now called the Franciscan Crown, or Seraphic Rosary. Many also say that this was the first time the second part of the modern Hail Mary was added: "Holy Mary, Mother of God, pray for us sinners, now and at the hour of our death." Now, this is the extra biblical part of the Hail Mary that makes many Protestants go crazy. But there is a beautiful reason for it.

MOTHER OF GOD

Mary is called the Theotokos, or "bearer," or "mother" of God. This does not refer to the transcendent God or the Trinity, but to God Incarnate as man in Jesus. We make this clear distinction in the current, third edition of the Creed. The first section refers to the eternal begottenness of the Son of God within the Trinity: "I believe in one Lord Jesus Christ, the Only Begotten Son of God, born of the Father before all ages. God from God, Light from Light, true God from true God, begotten, not made, consubstantial with the Father; Through him all things were made." It then goes on to profess the Incarnation of the Son through Mary in Jesus: "For us men and for our salvation he came down from heaven, and by the Holy Spirit was incarnate of the Virgin Mary, and became man."

The title of Mother of God was declared in the Council of Ephesus in 431 AD to emphasize the divinity and humanity of Jesus. It is really not about Mary, but about protecting the integrity of the Incarnation in Jesus. Most Catholics and Protestants actually agree on this.

The brief history of this title is interesting. St. Cyril (376–444 AD), the Patriarch of Alexandria, was trying to correct an error he saw in the teaching of Nestorius (386–451 AD), the powerful Patriarch of Constantinople. Nestorius was an intellectual and a conservative philosopher. People had tended to call Mary the Anthropotokos (Mother of Man) or the Theotokos. The name Theotokos was gaining ground. But Nestorius tended to look down his nose at the growing practice of the laity. He considered it rather crude popular devotion. So he proposed calling her the Christotokos, or "Mother of Christ."

Cyril of Alexandria saw the work of the Holy Spirit in this popular devotion and title. Today we call this the "sensus fidelium," or "sense of the faithful." This also had profound effects on the unity of the divine and human person of Jesus based on the Greek words for person. While conserving the apostolic tradition of the past, Cyril tended to be more forward looking, and Nestorius tended to be more conservative, to the exclusion of looking forward, or seeing the work of the Spirit in the faithful. It had far-reaching effects.

Cyril proposed using a rather novel philosophical term, "hypostatic union," based on the Greek υποστασισ (hypostasis), or "person," to describe the union of divinity and humanity in the one person of Jesus. This had already been used to describe the three "persons" in the Trinity. But it was rather new to describe the humanity and divinity of Jesus. Nestorius didn't like this; he considered it too novel. He preferred the use of the Greek word προσωπον (prosopon), or "face," to describe the divine and human aspect of Jesus. Cyril objected that it created two Jesuses, and mere appearances of divinity and humanity in him, which threatened the integrity of the fullness of the Incarnation. They debated in letters and homilies. Nestorius wouldn't budge. There was now a problem with one of the most powerful patriarchs in the Church being at odds with the growing practice of the majority of the faithful, and the development of theology among numerous bishops. The Church was in crisis.

Long story short: An ecumenical council was convened in Ephesus, a city alive with the new Marian devotion and large enough to accommodate such a gathering of bishops, to deliberate and decide. In the Council of Ephesus the Church adopted the language of the hypostatic union and the use of the title Theotokos for Mary in order to preserve the full integrity of the Incarnation. It was really all about Jesus. It was not about looking back and getting stuck in the past, but about preserving the past and moving forward.

PRAY FOR US

Asking the saints to pray for us has been practiced since the earliest days of the Church. We find such requests in the earliest known tombs of Christians in the Roman Empire. Scriptures also say the departed elders offer up the prayers of the saints before God (Rv 5:8). We are surrounded by a great "cloud of witnesses," which is the departed saints in Hebrews 12:1. And 2 Maccabees 12:42–46 describes the clear practice of praying for the faithful departed. Of course, there are also Scriptures that caution against communication with the dead while not following God in the now (1 Sm 28). But this continued exchange of love and intercessory prayer is part of our participation in the intercession of Jesus, who is the only ultimate intercessor by his own power (Heb 7:25; Jas 5:16). The beauty of love is that we are allowed to participate in that love in a way that even death cannot defeat. As St. Paul says to the Romans: "For I am convinced that neither death, nor life, nor angels, nor principalities, nor present things, nor future things, nor powers, nor height, nor depth, nor any other creature will be able to separate us from the love of God in Christ Jesus our Lord." (Rom 8:38–39)

Some say that we worship Mary like we worship God. But this is untrue. Two words are used for prayer in Latin: latria, which is reserved for worship of God, and dulia, which is used for saints. Even in Old English we "pray thee" when requesting something from another person. Hyperdulia was eventually used of Mary, as the Mother of Jesus.

But there are further developments in the Rosary as well. Along the way we began praying the Apostles' Creed, and various apparitions added short prayers that were attached to the main structure. Probably the biggest modern development is Blessed John Paul II's addition of the Luminous Mysteries to include more of the life of Christ between the Nativity and the Passion of Christ.

All of this brings out that the Rosary is a vibrant and living devotion that is completely focused on our participation in the life of Jesus, as modeled through Mary, his mother.

If we are aware of this rich history, even a brief version, it is impossible to rattle off a Hail Mary like we're calling out a horse race. It is too sacred and wonderful. Instead, we slow it down a bit, and pray the Rosary mindfully and prayerfully from the heart and soul, literally immersing ourselves in the unfathomable mystery of the Incarnation of the Logos, or Word in Jesus. We intuit beyond ideas and words our participation in this mystery through the ideas and words modeled in Mary's yes to this "wondrous love." We also immerse ourselves in the rich development of the Apostolic Church through the very prayers we pray. We know that we are part of something truly huge, universal, full, and Catholic.

So pull out your Rosary. Hold it in your hands for a few moments, and simply intuit the fullness of it. Feel the beads and the crucifix. Let it be sensual, soaking from your senses to your thoughts and imagination. Let it stir your emotions. Then settle with each breath to your deepest spirit. Let it permeate with the fullness of the divine Word incarnate into all that you are as a human being.

Then begin the formal prayers. Realize that they have a rich history and were not just arbitrarily thought up by someone. Pray them slowly, uniting them with your very breath. Breathe in the wonder of their meaning, and breathe out anything that is standing between you and a full communion with Jesus and his people.

Conclude by just sitting in silence. Experience the reality behind the Rosary that is beyond mere human words. There you will find the Logos, the Word. Then you will know Jesus, the Son of God and the Son of Mary.

2: THE JESUS PRAYER ROSARY

Now let's move to the Rosary of Eastern Christianity, the Jesus Prayer Rosary. Take a deep breath of the Spirit of God. Now breathe out anything not of the Spirit of God. Don't think it to death. You know what those things are; they are called sin. Now breathe out, and simply let go of anything standing between you and the Spirit of God. Relax for a moment. Settle in the Spirit, and let the Spirit settle deeply in your soul. Rest, and focus. Now we are ready to begin.

HISTORY

The modern Jesus Prayer began with the early Church. They wanted to follow St. Paul's injunction to "pray without ceasing." (1 Thes 5:17) The phrase "without ceasing" comes from one Greek word αδιαλειπτωσ (adialeiptos), with "a" meaning "not," "dia" meaning "with," and the root, λειπω (leipo), meaning "to leave." So adialeiptos literally means "not with leaving," or not to leave when praying. (Maybe we should tell that to the folks who leave right after Communion at Mass!) This means you should not let secular things interrupt your prayer. But how can we do that? We all have secular things to do during the day. Even monks have to make a living and make dinner. It does not mean we must pray constantly.

The early Church tried to figure out what that means. 1 Thessalonians 5:17 helps a bit by linking uninterrupted prayer with rejoicing and giving thanks. We can walk with an "attitude of gratitude," and be a person of praise. This turns us to God subconsciously at all times. But they still felt frustrated. They needed something that was more formal, but not intrusive in daily life.

In the fifth century two saints, Diadochos of Photiki and Hesychios the Priest, taught worshippers to unite the name and person of Jesus with every breath. Think about it. What's the one thing we do "without ceasing"? We breathe. (If you are not breathing please have someone call 911 right away!)

Through the years this practice developed into what we now call the Jesus Prayer. It is a specialized practice with Eastern Christian monks, and especially with the monks on Mount Athos, a monastic republic on a peninsula off the northeast coast of Greece. From there it has spread to the laity, and it is now practiced all around the world. Eastern monks even recognize that Western Christians can practice it with great benefit, though they emphasize that the full practice of Eastern Christianity is the best environment from which the prayer is prayed.

The full prayer goes like this: "Lord Jesus Christ, Son of God, have mercy on me, a sinner." Say that out loud a few times to learn it.

They also teach to unite the prayer with the breath. They unite the first part, "Lord Jesus Christ, Son of God," with the inhale, and the second part, "Have mercy on me, a sinner," with the exhale. Try it a few times.

Breathe in: "Lord Jesus Christ, Son of God"

Breathe out: "Have mercy on me, a sinner."

As we do this even for a few minutes we will begin to notice that the prayer naturally follows the physical act of breathing.

The first part of the prayer is positive, and the second part is negative. We breathe in all that is good and positive in Jesus and the Church, and we breathe out all that stands between us and a full communion with Jesus and the people of God in our families, the Church, and the folks of our daily life.

So breathe in the positive things of God: "Lord Jesus Christ, Son of God."

Now breathe out the negative things that stand between us and a full communion with God in Christ and the people of God: "Have mercy on me, a sinner." Do this a few more times, and settle into the positive and negative action of the prayer.

Now let's look at the specific words so we can gain a better understanding. But we do not want to get stuck obsessing over the meaning of the words while we pray. They will form an intuitive and almost subconscious base beneath the prayer as we pray. What is important is to let the prayer drop from the mind to the heart, or the very center of our being.

3: LORD

LORD

The first word in the Jesus Prayer is "Lord." It comes from YHWH, or the tetragrammaton, a Greek word meaning "the four letters," which is unpronounceable to emphasize that the fullness of God remains beyond comprehension or human speech. Names used in place of YHWH are Adonai, Jehovah, and Lord.

The Greek word is κύριος (*kyrios*), from κῦρος (*kuros*). It means "supreme in authority, controller, God, Lord, master." It is heard today in the Kyrie Eleison, or the "Lord, have mercy" that begins every Mass.

The Old English word for "lord" is hlafweard, which means the "maker," or "keeper of the bread." It is from the thirteenth century and the older feudal system that saved Europe from barbarianism after the fall of the Roman Empire. Hlaf means "loaf," and weard means "lord," or "master of a household, ruler, superior," also "God."

This is rich in significance. To call Jesus the Lord is to call him the "maker of the bread," and has Eucharistic overtones that also symbolize the process of our salvation in Christ.

CUTTING DOWN THE STALK

The first thing that we have to do in making bread is to cut down the stalk of wheat. You cannot get the grain of wheat unless it is separated from the stalk. It sounds obvious, but it is most important. The stalk is cut right at the base. It is not cut down because it is bad, but because it is good. We might say, "But I am a beautiful stalk of wheat!" (Imagine amber waves of grain, or a dancer moving gracefully as if in the wind.) "I am beautiful, and should not be cut down." But we must be cut down right at the base. We must give our whole life to Christ, and bring the old self to the cross in order to be born again through the dying and rising of Jesus. We bring the good and the bad: the sins that obviously need to go, and the righteousness that needs to be completed. We must bring it all.

Many think that they will postpone this more radical following of Jesus until the end of their life. But that is not what Jesus said. He called us to do it right from the start. He actually said that we cannot be his disciples unless we renounce everything and follow him. Anything less will not do. But most of us have families and a lot of responsibility. What does this renunciation really mean?

Jesus says that those who want to be his followers must renounce their possessions, relationships, and even their very selves (Lk 14:25–33). This is not because possessions, relationships, or our selves are bad, but because we often use them badly. Possessions often possess us, relationships are codependent and negatively enabling, and we settle for an incomplete version of ourselves that is nowhere near the fullness of what God created us to be. And this wrong use of right things often becomes so deeply ingrained in our daily habits that the only way to reestablish good patterns is through a complete break with the old ones that simply don't work. So we must let Jesus cut us down right at the base of our life. Then he can get to our wheat in order to make us into nourishing bread.

THRESHING

Next we have to separate the wheat from the cut stalks. We gather them into bunches and beat them on a tarp. This is called "threshing." It must be forceful enough to separate the wheat from the stalks, but not so violent as to destroy it.

Don't we sometimes feel a bit "threshed" in life? Yes! We may feel a bit beat up as hard times come one after the other. Sometimes they seem relentless. But they are necessary to separate the wheat from the stalk of our life.

But we do not have to go through this alone. We do this in groups, or community. The cut stalks of wheat are bunched together into groups just large enough to create the weight necessary for threshing, but not so large that it buffers the threshing and makes it impossible.

We also live in community. We have families, parishes, religious and ministry communities, and friends and coworkers, all of whom provide the support we need to make threshing effective but not destructive. Plus, sometimes it is actually the community that seems to create the threshing. But they are also the place that supports us through the hard times that separate the wheat from the stalk of our life.

WINNOWING

Next we must separate the wheat from the chaff (Mt 3:12). This is done through winnowing—throwing the wheat into the air and letting the wind separate the shell from the kernel, or grain, of wheat. The wind blows away the lighter shell from the heavier grain, which falls back onto the tarp.

Don't we feel a bit "up in the air" at times? Sure we do! We all face uncertain times. During the current financial crisis we all are uncertain about our future. Elderly folks wonder about their retirement. Young folks worry about an unimaginable national debt. I had to face the triple threat of being an older artist, the recession, and working in a Church that was facing bankruptcy in many of the dioceses I minster in.

But every crisis can be an opportunity when faced in Christ. We simply remodeled the way we ministered and began doing what we could do right where we were. It was hard work, especially at our age. But it worked better than anything I had ever done before.

Plus, I had taken a vow of poverty many years before. I have never sought to get rich by my ministry, nor should I. There are people in the Church who have vowed to make a lifestyle out of being "up in the air." They remind us all that regardless of the best-laid plans, we simply can never be certain about our future. Yes, we should plan responsibly, but it is God who is control.

The thing to remember is that the wind that separates the wheat from the chaff is the "wind of the Spirit." (Jn 3:8) It might be scary up in the air, but it is the Holy Spirit who is blowing us. Learn to ride the wind of the Spirit, be a bit spontaneous, and find new opportunities in every challenge. That is the way of the Spirit-led person. It is all about attitude. Learn to just ride the wind. Enjoy the adventure. It is coming whether we like it or not, so we might as well enjoy the journey.

GRINDING THE GRAIN

But we're not finished. Far from it! Our perfection in Christ is a process that takes our whole life. Just when we think we're getting the hang of riding the wind, it's time to come back to earth and get ground up.

Anyone who has ever been to Capernaum, in the Holy Land, has seen the huge grinding stone in the archaeological remains of that second-century seaside fisherman's village. It is a couple of meters across and nearly a meter wide. It weighs tons. It was used for grinding wheat into flour. The same thing must happen to the wheat of our life if we are to be made into bread.

Don't we ever feel a bit "ground up" by life? You bet we do! Sometimes the weight of life's pressures just seems too much to bear. But don't resist. Relax. Let yourself be ground into flour. Only then can we be turned into the dough that is used for the bread of Christ.

DOUGH

Once we become flour, then we can be made into dough. Mix in some water, salt, and a bit of yeast, and soon we are kneaded into dough. The water is the grace of God. The yeast rising is the Resurrection of Jesus. And let's face it, after being through tough times a bit of "kneading" feels pretty good. It's almost like a spiritual back rub. (A little to the left, please. Ah!)

So we get some reprieves along the way to being made into God's bread. The cross always leads to the Resurrection, and God never lets us be tempted beyond what we can handle. As St. Paul says, "No temptation has overtaken you except such as is common to man; but God is faithful, who will not allow you to be tempted beyond what you are able, but with the temptation will also make the way of escape, that you may be able to bear it." (1 Cor. 10:13)

RISING IN THE PAN

In modern baking the dough is placed in a pan. This can seem a bit restricting. We say, "But I like my shape just like I am!" But God never lets us stand still, or stay in the shape we have allowed ourselves to fall into. He loves us too much for that. Instead, we must allow ourselves to be conformed to the image of Christ. Conformed means to be "of one form."

Scripture says we are "to know him and the power of his resurrection and [the] sharing of his sufferings by being conformed to his death, if somehow I may attain the resurrection from the dead." (Phil 3:10–11) "We know that all things work for good for those who love God, who are called according to his purpose. For those he foreknew he also predestined to be conformed to the image of his Son, so that he might be the firstborn among many brothers." (Rom 8:28–29)

But now it's time to rise. It starts slowly, almost imperceptibly. Then we begin to really notice it. We say, "I'm rising! I've been through some tough times, but now I'm rising!"

Then what happens? Boom! We get poked, and we fall flat again. But that's OK. We say, "I'm a person of the resurrection, and greater is He who is in me than he who is in the world." (1 Jn 4:4) "And in Christ I have overcome the world." (Jn 16:33) Then again, bang! We're poked and deflated, and we fall flat again. In the normal baking process that happens three times. Why? If we don't get "poked" we stay filled with hot air, and when we get put into the oven we blow up. Many say that as a preacher I am filled not always with the Spirit, but with hot air.

Yes, I need to be poked to keep my head from expanding too much with "hot air" instead of the Holy Spirit.

THE OVEN

Lastly, we get put into the oven. And it's hot as Hades in there—or at least purgatory! But you cannot become bread without going through the baking process, and that means being put into the oven. There's simply no way around it.

That's true with us too. Life can get pretty hot. Do any of us reading this book have trouble with anger? Who doesn't? We get frustrated when we do not let go of our agendas and let God's agenda unfold. Frustration leads to anger. Then the temper flares, whether we let people see it or not. Anger tends to blind us to the will of God. That heat can keep us from calmly discerning God's real agenda.

Or maybe just the nonstop pace of fending off the challenges and crises of life seems a tad too hot. Sometimes life can seem like an oven, or worse yet, a pressure cooker.

These things are going to happen whether we like it or not. Most are beyond our control. If we relax, we will discover that Jesus is just baking us into a golden brown loaf of warm bread that can nourish a hungry world. We will be nourished as well.

CONCLUSION

So the first word of the Jesus Prayer, "Lord," is all-inclusive. It is filled with the process of the continual dying and rising of Jesus in our life that allows us to let go of the old self that doesn't work very well and rise up as a new creation in Christ, as the person God really created us to be. So don't be afraid. Let yourself be baked into a nourishing loaf of bread by God. Let go of trying to be your own lord. Believe me, the task is beyond you, and beyond me. Let Jesus really be the Lord of your life.

4: JESUS

The next word in the Jesus Prayer is "Jesus." It comes from the Greek ιησουσ *(Iesous)* and the Hebrew י.עושוה *(y hosua)* or עשׂוה.י *(Yhowshua or Jehoshua)*, and means "YHWH saves," or simply "salvation." It is the same name given to Joshua the son of Nun, the Prophet Hosea, and Jesus ben Sirach (Yeshua [Jesus], son of Eleazar, son of Sira [50:27]), the author of the book of Ecclesiasticus. It is also the name given to Jesus Christ.

We use the words *salvation* and *savior* constantly. We find them all throughout Scripture and Liturgy. Yet, we use them so much that they often lose their power. More completely, salvation means to be open, wide, free, safe; or to avenge, defend, deliver, help, preserve, rescue; to be safe, to save, and to have victory. It is a wonderfully rich word filled with freedom, openness, safety, victory, and salvation. To be saved is to be filled with joy.

Perhaps the only folks in modern times who really "get" salvation are the 12-step program brothers and sisters. And what is the first step? The first step is to admit that we are totally powerless and need a higher power to be saved. How many of us have tried to follow Jesus and be good members of the Church by our own power? How many of us have failed repeatedly using human efforts alone? I have too! It is only with the power of the Holy Spirit that I can even begin to follow Jesus.

Jesus was most clear that human effort alone is not enough. He said that we would evangelize the entire world, but that we need the power of the Spirit to do so. "And he said to them, Thus it is written that the Messiah would suffer and rise from the dead on the third day and that repentance, for the forgiveness of sins, would be preached in his name to all the nations, beginning from Jerusalem. You are witnesses of these things. And [behold] I am sending the promise of my Father upon you; but stay in the city until you are clothed with power from on high." (Lk 24:46–49) "But you will receive power when the Holy Spirit comes upon you, and you will be my witnesses in Jerusalem, throughout Judea and Samaria, and to the ends of the earth." (Acts 1:8)

It has been said that we cannot really understand salvation until we have reached our point of despair, when we realize we alone do not have the ability to get out of our lost state. Until that point is reached we will still try to save ourselves with the best of intentions. Have you ever really despaired of the ability to succeed? I have. That point is different for everyone, but it is real. I cannot impose my point of despair on someone else, or vice versa. That would be judgment, and it is a dangerous road. So what is it? It is the point where we are overcome with the realization that we need God's power to continue. And that is the beauty of salvation. God's power is available through the Spirit, and especially through the life, death, and the Resurrection of Jesus.

I had a friend who used to lead rafting tours on the great rivers of the American West. One day they were hit by a flash flood. The water rose quickly, and soon they knew they were in trouble. The rising water had forced the rattlesnakes out of their holes by the banks, so the riverbank was lined with them, making it impossible for the whole group to walk out. But someone had to go. Someone had to take the risk. My friend decided that he would go. So he mustered up some courage, ran up the bank, narrowly missing being bitten, and went for help. But he was gone a long time. The hours slipped by as the water rose. Soon the rafters tied off on some tree limbs protruding from a submerged island. But the rising water was covering even the trees. At that point they really thought they were going to die. They had reached their point of despair.

It was just at that point that they saw the helicopters. My friend had found help, and they were coming just in time. They lifted the exhausted and terrified rafters onto the helicopters and flew them to safety, only a few minutes away by air. Hours of fear had been suddenly relieved by a few minutes of salvation. These folks knew what it meant to be saved.

St. Bonaventure once said that we are like people who have fallen into a deep and desperately dark pit. Try as we might to climb out by own power, we repeatedly fall back to the bottom. Sometimes we might even get to the very top and think we can pull ourselves out, but then we lose our grip or footing and fall all the way to the bottom of the pit again. Only Jesus can get us out. He reaches down with loving, strong hands and a firm grip, and he pulls us out of the pit into the daylight again. We have to cooperate. But it is his power that lifts us out.

How does Jesus do this? In Scripture he says, "No one has greater love than this, to lay down one's life for one's friends." (Jn 15:13) Jesus lays down his life for us. He also says, "I am the good shepherd, and I know mine and mine know me, just as the Father knows me and I know the Father; and I will lay down my life for the sheep." (Jn 10:14–15)

It is like a parent who tells her child, "Do not play in the street." But in the heat of the game the child chases the ball into the street anyway. The child does not see the traffic, but the parent does. So the parent runs into the street, pushes the child out of the way, gets hit by an oncoming car, and dies. Isn't that the great love of any good parent for her child? Of course it is. You all know this love for your children. The child does not understand what has just happened. But when he is older he will be stunned by the love of his parent for him.

That is what Jesus does for us, and he does so personally. It is no mere metaphor. It is real. And it is personal. We deserve to die, but he died in our place so that we might live. And the wonder of it is that he rose from the dead in order to prove the absolute victory of such love over death. At first we are moved by this act of love, but as we grow we begin to realize what wondrous love this really is. Jesus loves us. It is real and wondrous, and it is personal.

Once we do this, the slate is washed clean. We are forgiven, and we are free. How many of us have sinned? All of us! But how many have ever been forgiven? Some have, but not all. Forgiveness opens us up to a freedom that is unbelievable and underserved. It is grace, a gift. When we are forgiven it feels like the weight of the cosmos has been lifted from our shoulders. We were stooped from the weight. We could not rise and walk, but we could not sleep when lying down. It was hell, right here on earth. Forgiveness frees us from the weight and the constant burden that unforgivingness brings. That is why in Scripture forgiveness is called the "power of the keys." (Mt 16:19; 18:18) When we forgive or withhold forgiveness we release or bind others and ourselves. When we are forgiven we can forgive. We rise up and walk; we run without getting weary. That is what it means to be saved.

There is a little monk who walks around Mount Athos and asks the pilgrims, "What do you think, brother, are we being saved," and after pausing he poignantly adds, "today?" It is not about yesterday, or really even about the next time you go to church. It is about today. It is here and now. Salvation was accomplished two thousand years ago on Calvary. But it must be experienced every day. And we grow in our understanding of salvation day in and day out. Real salvation is never far from that first moment of realizing what it truly means to be saved, and saved through the dying and rising of Jesus. It is personal, folks! And it is intimate. And if we walk with a daily appreciation of it, we will never stray too far from the course God has for each of us.

Think about it. Jesus gave his life for us long ago on Calvary. But we must respond to his sacrifice daily. Plus, for those who fully understand the Eucharist, the ancient bloodshed of Jesus on Calvary is sacramentally repeated and extended from long ago to right now, this very day. It is not some distant event from long ago. It is right now, today. And it is personal.

Salvation is not one-sided. It is about a personal love relationship with Jesus, and it must be mutual. Jesus initiates it, but we must respond with grace. Every day we have a decision to make: Will I rise up and follow Jesus today? I was saved yesterday, but will I continue in salvation today? The choice is ours. Are we being saved today?

This is the real meaning of the name Jesus. What about, it brothers and sisters? Are we being saved . . . today?

5: CHRIST

The next word in the Jesus Prayer is "Christ." It simply means "anointed." It comes from the Greek Χριστός, or *Christos*. It is the Greek version used for the Messiah (חי.שׁ.מ., *masiyah*) and applied to Jesus as the "Christ."

Followers of Jesus are called Christians (from the Greek χριστιανοσ, *Christianos*). It comes from Acts 11:26, and it is used for followers of Jesus in Antioch. It is also used in 1 Peter 4:16 for enduring sufferings with Christ. Some have also said that it means "like Christ."

But what does Christos, or Christ, really mean? What does it mean to be anointed by the Spirit? Is it enough to just be excited, or is there something deeper, something more?

We are to be anointed like Christ: "But the one who . . . anointed us is God." (2 Cor 1:21) The word for "anointed" here is the Greek χριω (*chrio*), which is akin to χραομαι (*chraomai*), meaning "to make ready for use," "rubbed or smeared with oil," or "to consecrate to an office or religious service." This is powerful, for it means that both Jesus and his followers are to literally be "smeared" with the Spirit. We are also "rubbed," which implies something that is repeated. We are to be rubbed through and through with the Spirit of God before we are ready for ministry. And it will happen throughout our life and ministry in Christ. There will be deepening and growth.

I come from the Jesus movement, which was largely Pentecostal and charismatic in nature. When I became a Roman Catholic I entered through the monastic/Franciscan, patristic, and charismatic doorways into the Church. The Catholic Charismatic Renewal was a point of contemporary commonality for me. I have been a part of the Renewal since 1978, when I transitioned from Christian Contemporary Music to more Catholic venues across the country and began encountering Charismatic prayer groups. I have also been a part of the Southern California Renewal Communities (SCRC) since 1978, when they first asked me to minister during their convention, and I have gone back every two or three years since.

But as a Catholic charismatic I am intensely aware of one thing: Sometimes we think we're anointed, but we're only excited! Many well-meaning, excited, but seriously misguided religious folks head off in wrong directions all the time. It brings out religious fanaticism instead of genuine radicalism. Radicalism is rooted, like a radish (from Late Latin *radicalis*, "of or having roots," from Latin *radix*, "root"). It allows a plant to grow high and strong to face the worst winds because its roots are deep and balanced. Fanaticism just mimics certain external aspects of genuine radicalism without really understanding their roots and essential meaning. It has no roots, so it is easily blown away by the coming storms that inevitably challenge any spiritual life. It is worth noting that *The Didache*, which first condemns abortion in the late first and early second centuries, also condemns religious fanaticism as destructive. "Likewise refrain from fanaticism, quarrelling, and hot-temperedness, for these too can breed homicide." (Didache 3)

It is a well-known fact that unruly emotions and passions can blind us to the truth that sets us free. This is sometimes called "emotionalism," and it is a bad thing. How many of us can rightly discern when we are angry or overly elated? These emotions stir up the pond of our soul so that the waters become murky as the sediment is disturbed. We must let the waters of our soul settle before they can become clear again. Emotionalism blinds us to the truth and clear vision.

Yet enthusiasm and passion is a good thing if used the right way. The word *enthusiasm* simply means "in God, *en-theos*," or "in essence or being, *en-ousia*." Plus the height of the ministry of Jesus Christ is called the Passion. His death was not some passionless, robotic acceptance of death and rising. No. Jesus went through the whole human experience. He was fully alive, and experienced the physical, emotional, and spiritual pain profoundly. So the trick is to use our enthusiasm and passions well. We are to live with passion, to be enthusiastic. Being enthusiastic means emotions are used the right way, to empower us for the good things of God.

The Scriptures give us a very clear description of what the real anointed person is like. St. Paul writes beautifully when he says, "the fruit of the Spirit is love, joy, peace, patience, kindness, generosity, faithfulness, gentleness, self-control. Against such there is no law. Now those who belong to Christ [Jesus] have crucified their flesh with its passions and desires. If we live in the Spirit, let us also follow the Spirit. Let us not be conceited, provoking one another, envious of one another." (Gal 5:22–26)

Who does not want these beautiful fruits in their life? They are indeed what every human heart hungers for deep inside. The trouble is that we are so out of touch with ourselves that we sometimes don't even know that this is what we are hungry for. The waters of our spiritual pond are so agitated that we cannot even see what's really inside our soul.

The way we get free of that is in verses 24 and 25: "Now those who belong to Christ [Jesus] have crucified their flesh with its passions and desires. If we live in the Spirit, let us also follow the Spirit." As St. Paul says elsewhere, "you have taken off the old self with its practices and have put on the new self, which is being renewed, for knowledge, in the image of its creator." (Col 3:9, 10) And Jesus says, "If any one comes to me without hating his father and mother, wife and children, brothers and sisters, and even his own life, he cannot be my disciple. Whoever does not carry his own cross and come after me cannot be my disciple." (Lk 14:26–27)

What this means is that we let the "old self" die through the cross of Jesus. You know the old self. It's the "us" that doesn't really make us—or anyone else—all that happy. Then we can be "born again," (Jn 3:4) and raised up a new person (2 Cor 5:17) according to the image that God originally created us to be: one who is happy, blessed, and fulfilled.

Let's look briefly at these fruits of the Spirit:

Love in Greek is αγαπη (*agape*). It is one of three words used for love in Christianity. All three mean "self-emptying," or loving for the sake of another. In this case "another" is God, other people, and God's creation. When we stop being obsessed with self-fulfillment, then we can really be fulfilled. As Jesus says, "Whoever wishes to come after me must deny himself, take up his cross, and follow me. For whoever wishes to save his life will lose it, but whoever loses his life for my sake will find it." (Mt 16:24–25)

Joy is from the Greek χαρα (*chara*) and means "cheerfulness, calm delight." It is not some giddy or superficial joy. It is a deep-set joy that transcends both the good and bad external things that come our way. Like Jesus, this joy can weep with those who weep, and rejoice with those who rejoice (Rom 12:15). It comes from a death of the old self so that a new, caring person can have joy and bring it to others.

Peace comes from the Greek ειρηνη (*eirene*); it means "to rest in quiet, to join or unite with." To rest in peace means to let the old self die so that a new person can arise in us through the dying and rising of Jesus.

Patience comes from μακροθυμια (*makrothymia*), and it means "to be slow in avenging wrongs." When the old, ego-attached self dies with Christ, then our true self in Christ can rise up and seek not vengeance, but justice and peace.

Kindness comes from χρηστοτησ (*chrestotes*) and means "to seek the morally useful and most excellent thing gently." It is not forced or coerced externally. It is not obsessive. It is gentle but strong.

Goodness, or generosity, is from αγαθωσυνη (*agathosyne*); it means "that which is good, honorable, virtuous, and upright." It is something that can be done in the daylight and shouted from the rooftops; there is no need to cover it up or be ashamed of it. Most of our old selves had a lot that we did not want other people to know about. Real goodness can be an open book before God and others. After all, in heaven we will "know as we are known." There will be no secrets in the eternal.

Faith comes from πιστισ (*pistis*). We just had a Year of Faith in the Catholic Church in 2011. Faith is the ability to believe the unbelievable. It can see what the world cannot see. Scripture says, "Faith is the realization of what is hoped for and evidence of things not seen. " (Heb 11:1) The word *realization* in Greek is υποστασισ (*hypostasis*), and it means "substance, essence." It is the same for the hypostatic union of the divine and human in the one person of Jesus. It is also used of the three persons of the Trinity. Faith is the very personification, or substance, of things hoped for. It is what Mary had when she believed the message of the angel Gabriel at the Annunciation, when she was told something that was too much to understand with human logic alone. She did not understand, but she believed, and because of that Jesus was born into her life, and through her life into our world. As St. Paul writes, "We walk by faith, not by sight." (2 Cor 5:7)

Gentleness is from πραυτησ (*prautes*), and it means "mild, meek." Moses was meek, but he was not a coward. He could stand up to Pharaoh because the one greater than Pharaoh was with him. Meek does not mean mousy. It means we depend fully on God for our strength, and do not rely on our own strength alone.

Chastity comes from εγκρατεια (*egkrateia*) and means simply "self-control." But this self-control cannot be exercised without God. Otherwise it becomes a "law," even though it is a new set of laws. The most important thing to remember is that we cannot do it ourselves. We must learn to cooperate with grace in order for it to be fully effective in our lives. Chastity has a special significance in an era when promiscuity and sexual confusion are quickly becoming the norm. Like Lot of old, we must leave behind the Sodom and Gomorrah of our promiscuous Western culture—without looking back, like Lot's wife, lest we be destroyed in that lust that turned them into pillars of salt and that is less than fully human. We must turn from the unchastity of the secular world and embrace the way of Jesus according to our state of life as celibate, single, or married persons. Only then will we be truly fulfilled as complete and healthy persons in Christ.

There are other Scriptures we can look at to see what the authentic life of the Spirit really is. It is nothing short of becoming like Jesus, as "little Christs," or Christians. We could look to the Sermon on the Mount, which is said to be the heart of the New Testament, especially the Beatitudes. We could look to the great love chapter, 1 Corinthians 13. These all point to what Jesus was really like as a human person. And we could look to the great anointing Scripture that describes his life and ministry. Quoting Isaiah, Jesus said, "The Spirit of the Lord is upon me, because he has anointed me to bring glad tidings to the poor. He has sent me to proclaim liberty to captives and recovery of sight to the blind, to let the oppressed go free, and to proclaim a year acceptable to the Lord." (Lk 4:18, 19)

So a good definition of Christian is "like Jesus," the Christos, the anointed one. We all seek to be like the person of persons, who shows us what it is like to really be human again. But we can only be like Jesus if we let go of the old self that made us and everyone else so unhappy, and become a new person conformed to the image of Jesus.

6: SON OF GOD

"Son of God" is the next phrase in the Jesus Prayer. The Greek is pretty straightforward: *Son* is υιοσ (*huios*) and means simply "son." θεοσ (*theos*) refers to any deity; it is used of the one God. It is interesting to note that God's name is not actually God, but remains ה.וה.י (YHWH), and is beyond full human comprehension and utterance. The most common early word from which we get "God" in the Old Testament is א.ה.ים (*elohiym*), which is both neuter and plural, implying why God can refer to his being as "us" in creating humanity in his image (Gn 1:26). In English we use simply "Lord," as we discussed previously.

TRINITY

"Son of God" is far from simplistic. It is a phrase rich and deep when correctly understood. It includes the notion of the eternally begotten Son of God, the Incarnation of the Son of God, the continued Incarnation in the Church, and the sacraments, specifically the Eucharist. So this simple phrase is indicative of the fullness, or catholicity, of our faith in Jesus Christ.

There is a difference between being begotten and being incarnate. One is going on all the time, throughout eternity.

The other takes place in space and time. Let's first look at the notion of being eternally begotten.

The creeds are always a helpful point of reference. We use what is popularly called the Nicene Creed in most of our churches. But it is a later adaptation of the Nicene Creed of 325 AD that was promulgated in Constantinople, in 381 AD.

The version of the Nicene Creed in the Roman Catholic Church that most of us grew up with said:

> We believe in one Lord, Jesus Christ,
> the only Son of God,
> eternally begotten of the Father,
> God from God, Light from Light,
> true God from true God,
> begotten, not made, one in Being
> with the Father.
> Through him all things were made.

This is nice, and it says things correctly. But it is not a precise or formally equivalent translation of the Greek or Latin, so we were given the third edition of *The New Roman Missal* in 2011. This is an opportunity to look at the original more deeply.

The newest version says:

> I believe in one Lord Jesus Christ,
> the Only Begotten Son of God,
> born of the Father before all ages.
> God from God, Light from Light,
> true God from true God,
> begotten, not made, consubstantial
> with the Father;
> Through him all things were made.

The newer text is truer to both the original Greek and the Latin translation of it. While every word of the creed has deep significance and was carefully chosen, there are some key words that are important for us here.

The Greek μονογενῆ (*monogene*), meaning "the only member of a kin." *Begotten* comes from the Greek γεννάω (*gennao*); it means "born of," usually referring to the father rather than the mother. πατρός (*patros*), or "father," is specifically used, so we know Jesus is the "only begotten" Son of the Father.

The phrase "before all ages" means simply "before all time," or in the realm of eternity. The Greek πρό (*pro*) means "before" and often refers to time. So this means before time in eternity. Theologically, we would say "eternally begotten."

Made comes from the Greek ποιηθέντα (*poiethenta*) and means "brought into existence." So for the Son to be "begotten, not made," means that he proceeds eternally, but does not come into existence.

Consubstantial comes from the Greek ὁμο-ούσιος (*homoousios*); it simply means "one in"- "essence, being, substance."

There could be confusion between *begotten* and *made* in the strict sense of the Greek words, so the actual Nicene Creed of 325 AD adds a helpful explanation at the conclusion: "But those who say: 'There was a time when he was not;' and 'He was not before he was made;' and 'He was made out of nothing,' or 'He is of another substance' or 'essence,' or 'The Son of God is created,' or 'changeable,' or 'alterable'—they are condemned by the holy catholic and apostolic Church."

If your head is spinning a bit, don't worry, so was mine! What this means is that the notion of the "Son of God" refers first to his place in the Trinity, where he is eternally being begotten of the Father. There was never a time when he was not being begotten, and there will never be a time when he is not begotten. It is an eternal process denoting eternal relationship. And it is wonderful.

St. Augustine uses the analogy of a candle before water. The instant the light of the candle exists, it is reflected in the water. In his thinking, before modern science there was no time lag. It was instantaneous. Likewise, as the Father exists, he is immediately reflected in the Son. The Father is eternal, and so is the Son. You cannot have one without the other. The same thing could be applied to the Spirit regarding procession.

The Trinity is one of the mysteries of the Orthodox Christian Faith. It is referred to clearly in Scripture, but it isn't theologically explained. It came from the generations of the Church that also compiled the New Testament, so the Trinity and the New Testament are intrinsically connected and interdependent. Those who claim to disprove the Trinity using the New Testament inadvertently deny the authority of the New Testament they are quoting from. To believe in the New Testament is also to believe in the Trinity, both of which are defined by the Church Jesus established. It's somewhat of a "chicken or the egg" scenario.

The Trinity and the Incarnation have never changed. But our understanding of them does develop. It took hundreds of years for the Church to come to an essential agreement regarding the fundamental, or foundational, understandings of both. And they are still developing (but not changing) today.

It is said that St. Bonaventure referred to the Trinity as a self-evident doctrine if we believe in God's transcendence, goodness, and love. We often take such things for granted, so let's see what he might mean.

To be transcendent is to be "above" all things of the created world. It implies self-existence. In other words, God is above all things, and needs nothing to exist.

But God is also good and loving. Goodness means that God is diffusive to another. Love is the union of at least two in order to generate new life in a third. But God is one. So how can he be diffusive to another within himself? How can he join two to bring forth new life in at least a third if he is one, and he is transcendent? If God must create to fulfill these clear divine attributes, then he is not God, but only *a* god. God fulfills all of this within his one existence in a perfect mystery of goodness, love, and transcendence.

Now, do you really understand that? No! And neither do I. It is not meant to be fully understood. It is perfect logic that defies human comprehension. It is meant to elicit awe and wonder at the mystery of it.

Many of us remember hearing the story of St. Augustine and the Trinity when we were young. When St. Augustine was the Bishop of Hippo, in Northern Africa, he was delivering a series of sermons on the Trinity. Between sermons he would stroll along the beach to contemplate and rest his mind. On one of his walks he met a young boy who had dug a hole in the sand and was repeatedly filling buckets of water from the sea to empty them into the hole. Augustine's curiosity was stirred, so he asked the boy what he was doing. The little boy responded, "I am going to take that big ocean and put it in this little hole." The wise Bishop Augustine said, "Son, that ocean is too big to fit in that little hole." The little boy immediately said, "Well, it's a lot easier for me to put that big ocean into that little hole than for you to put the big Trinity into your little mind, Bishop Augustine!" At that the little boy disappeared, and Bishop Augustine knew that he had been visited by an angel to remind him of the limitations of even the best theology.

This returns us to one of the main descriptive names of God in the Old Testament, the Hebrew word אֱלֹהִים (lohiym), which is both plural and neuter. As God says in creating Adam, "Let us make man in our image." (Gn 1:26) "Us"? Yes! Already in the first chapters of Genesis the Trinity is being revealed in part.

INCARNATION

"Son of God" also implies the Incarnation of the eternally begotten Word through Mary as a human being. The Nicene Creed doesn't stop with the eternally begotten Son of God, but goes on to say:

> For us men and for our salvation
> he came down from heaven,
> and by the Holy Spirit was incarnate
> of the Virgin Mary,
> and became man.

As previously discussed, Mary is called the Theotokos, or the bearer, or Mother of God. The Word was made flesh.

Incarnation comes from the Greek σαρκωθέντα, from the root σαρξ (*sarx*), and means simply "in flesh," or "meat." Think about when you order red meat from the Mexican food place. What do you order? Carne. That's right—they come from the same root words.

But imagine that—the fullness of divinity taking on flesh, that which is beyond limitation taking on the limitations of human being and flesh. Of the simplicity of God St. Bonaventure said, "He is the mystical Sphere, both the Center and the Circumference, the Center which is everywhere, and the Circumference is nowhere." If that is not mystery enough, this reality then takes on flesh in Jesus. He is within flesh yet not enclosed, the servant but also the master, lowly yet above all things, poor but the king of kings, chaste but the bridegroom of the Church and spouse of all, obedient but the ruler of all.

This also gives us the reason for our love of Mary, his mother. We already touched on Mary in our treatment of the Marian Rosary. But it is good to remind ourselves here as well. She is the Mother of the Son of Man and the Son of God in one Christ. She is highly venerated due to our focus on the mystery of the Incarnation, but only Jesus is worshipped as God. We look to her, but she always points us to Jesus, and when we look to Jesus as the Word incarnate we cannot help but be moved to veneration of Mary. "Bonaventure adopts the well-known distinction between the worship of latria, owed only to God, that of dulia, given to the saints, and what is called hyperdulia, that is, the veneration owed to the Mother of the Lord, which is greater than simple dulia." (Gambero, Luigi. *Mary in the Middle Ages*. San Francisco: Ignatius Press, 2010. Kindle edition.) We give her *dulia* and even *hyperdulia*, but offer Jesus only *latria*, or worship due God. All of this is because of our awe and wonder for the Incarnation of the eternally begotten Son of God in Jesus Christ.

THE CHURCH

But we are also told that the Incarnation of the Son of God continues in the Church. We are the "body of Christ." (Rom 12:13) St. Paul says, "Now you are Christ's body, and individually parts of it." (1 Cor 12:27) We are Christians, "like Christ," or as some have said, "little Christs." Likewise, we are Catholics, or "universally and fully" like Christ. But this is not fully embodied in any one Christian. Rather, it takes the unity of the body of Christ to fully manifest that wonderful reality. That reality is the Church.

Scripture encourages us not to "absent ourselves from the assembly, as some do." (Heb 10:25) And already in the time of Scripture, the early Church faced schism and heresy. This problem continued in the early Church, and the writings of the earliest Church fathers address it. Clement of Rome, *The Didache*, the Letters of Ignatius of Antioch, Irenaeus of Lyons, and even Tertullian address the problem of division by appealing to the apostolic leadership of bishops, who succeeded from the apostles or from their immediate successors. This is called "apostolic succession." Plus, when there was a dispute between various bishops and they could not reach a peaceful unanimity, they appealed to the Bishop of Rome as the successor to St. Peter to preside in love and bring unity in Christ.

But this is also very personal. It means that we must find unity in Christ through the mediation of the Church when we face various divisive issues with other members of the Church. This is not just about big ideas relegated to popes and bishops to deliberate. It is about us, about you and me. It is about bringing Jesus into the little things of life according to the teaching of the gospel, which comes to us through the Church. (Lk 16:10)

As I mentioned earlier, in concert I often use a popular song from my repertoire called "St. Theresa's Prayer." The lyrics say:
Christ has no body now, but yours.
No hands, no feet on earth, but yours.
Yours are the eyes through which he looks compassion on this world.
Yours are the feet with which he walks to do good.
Yours are the hands with which he blesses all the world.

While I sing I have the audience hold hands and meditate on the fact that they are holding the hand of Jesus. You cannot give Jesus without religious self-righteousness until you can receive the hand of Jesus from everyone, even those who do not believe in him. This is quite a trick! Mother Teresa of Calcutta said that she could see the face of Jesus in the face of every poor person, whether they believed in him or not. Only then could she give Jesus to anyone without pride or religious self-righteousness.

Can we see the hand of Jesus in our spouse, our family, our brother and sister Catholics and Christians, our employers and employees? That's where the big stuff is tested. And until we can begin to really find Jesus there, we should not expect to bring him to the big issues of our modern world.

When we can learn to do this, we begin to experience the miracle of becoming the continuing Incarnation of the Son of God in the Church.

THE EUCHARIST

But it does not stop here. We also learn to find the continuing Incarnation of the Son of God in the Eucharist. The early Church understood this clearly. The Scriptures call the Eucharist the body of Christ too. Extending John 6 and the Eucharistic texts of the synoptic Gospels, St. Paul testifies about the Eucharistic tradition he received when he says, "The cup of blessing that we bless, is it not a participation in the blood of Christ? The bread that we break, is it not a participation in the body of Christ? Because the loaf of bread is one, we, though many, are one body, for we all partake of the one loaf." (1 Cor 10:16–17) There is a clear connection between the Church being the body of Christ and the Eucharist we receive together being the body of Christ.

The early Church was also clear about this. St. Ignatius of Antioch connected those who abstained from the Eucharist with those who denied Jesus's full Incarnation in the flesh. He was fighting the Docetists, who denied the full humanity of Jesus. For Ignatius the belief that the body and blood of Jesus was fully present in the Eucharistic elements was a sacramental way of stating clearly through sacred mystery, beyond mere human words, the reality of the Incarnation.

The same is true today. When we celebrate the Eucharist we are saying through sacrament, or sacred mystery, the full truth of the Incarnation of the Word, the Son of God, in Jesus Christ. Plus, we are receiving Jesus, not just as Spirit, but as incarnation, body and blood, soul and divinity, under the appearance of physical elements of bread and wine. We are literally receiving the incarnate Christ into every part of our being, spirit, soul, and body through the Eucharist. Jesus physically and spiritually courses through every fiber of our being. When we understand this we are left in awe and wonder at every gathering of the Church to celebrate the Eucharist as the "source and summit" of our Christian life.

CONCLUSION

So the simple words *Son of God* are far from simplistic. They include the major mysteries of the Catholic and Orthodox

Christian faith. And they are stated in the wordless intuition of breathing in: Lord, Jesus Christ, Son of God.

So let's take a moment and simply breathe in these words. But instead of obsessing about their meaning, let's just intuit the deeper reality of the words, and let them soak in with each breath. Breathe in the fullness of all that is wonderful in Jesus, the Church, and our salvation and redemption in him. Allow yourself to be in full communion with Jesus, the Church, and the sacraments, especially the Eucharist. Now breathe out, and let go of anything that is keeping you from that full communion. Again, do not obsess about sin. Simply let go of anything standing between you and these wonderful things of God. It's as easy as breathing in and breathing out!

7: HAVE MERCY

Lord, Jesus Christ, Son of God, *have mercy* . . .

With the Jesus Prayer we breathe in the first part of the prayer and breathe out the second part. Now that we have reviewed the first part, it is time to move to the second. Breathing in is literally filling up with air, and breathing out is letting go. It is very physical, and reflects a deeper spiritual movement. We breathe out air with the words *have mercy*. We begin to let go of anything standing between us and God through Jesus, between us and a full communion with the people of God in the Church, and between us and our families, or the best part of the secular world.

The word *mercy* has both Hebrew and Greek roots. There are several Hebrew words used for it. The most well-known word is חֶסֶד (*hesed*), which means "kindness, pity toward"; it's used to describe kindness, loving-kindness, goodness, favor, good, goodliness, and pity. The "mercy seat" is most important in the Jewish ritual worship mentioned in Exodus 25:17–22. The word is כַּפֹּרֶת (*kapporet*), which means "the lid that covered the Ark of the Covenant," and God dwells there in the Law. Jesus is the mercy seat, or "propitiation," or ιλαστηριον (*hilasterion*), in Romans 3:25 for the follower of Jesus. The last Hebrew word is found in Psalm 51 for deep, heartfelt, and contrite repentance to God. The word is חָנַן (*hanan*), which means "to bend or stoop in kindness to an inferior; to favor, bestow." It can also mean "gracious, merciful, supplication, favor, pity, fair."

The Greek words for "mercy" are ελεεω (*eleeo*) and ελεοσ (*eleos*). They are related to the familiar Kyrie Eleison, or the "Lord, have mercy" used at Mass, and are repeated frequently in the Divine Liturgy of the Christian East. Scholars say that this includes a compassion that encompasses not only sympathy but also empathy. The Greek ιλαστηριον (*hilasterion*) is also used for "merciful"; it means "the atoning victim who will bear the full weight of punishment for the sins of another." The tax collector cries out for this mercy in the parable of the Pharisee and the tax collector, in Luke 18:9–14. After the crucifixion and Resurrection for Christians, Jesus *is* this mercy and propitiation. (1 Jn 1:2)

All of the words and scholarly teaching on them indicate that *mercy* means both sympathy and empathy that are deeply compassionate. We are instructed to be "of one mind, sympathetic, loving toward one another, compassionate, humble." (1 Pt 3:8) Being sympathetic means being compassionate from the outside in. It is most wonderful and challenging, and if we would show such sympathy for one another, it would change the world.

But empathy is something far more. It means compassion from the inside out. Having empathy means walking a mile in someone else's shoes. It means getting right inside the people we care about, and understanding them from the inside out. We know *why* they are both good and bad. We understand their motivations for their words and actions. It is intimate and personal, and pretty difficult for most of us to do with one another.

I would maintain that it is actually impossible to do. Even with married couples of many years, there remains a certain part of their spouse that is beyond their understanding.

Not only that, sometimes we do not even understand ourselves. St. Paul writes to the Romans, "For I do not understand my own actions. For I do not do what I want, but I do the very thing I hate." (Rom 7:15) This could easily lead us to despair. We do not control, much less really even know ourselves. But there is an answer. St. Paul continues, "Wretched man that I am! Who will deliver me from this body of death? Thanks be to God through Jesus Christ our Lord!" (Rom 7:24–25)

St. Augustine builds on this in a way that is remarkable. In his famous poem "Late Have I Loved Thee," he simply says, "You were within me, but I was outside." He begins by saying, "Urged to reflect upon myself, I entered under your guidance the innermost places of my being; but only because you had become my helper was I able to do so. I entered, then, and with the vision of my spirit, such as it was, I saw the incommutable light far above my spiritual ken and transcending my mind."

God knows us better than we know ourselves because he is closer to us than we are to ourselves. Think about it. No one knows a person but the spirit of a person. As St. Paul writes to the Corinthians: "this God has revealed to us through the Spirit. For the Spirit scrutinizes everything, even the depths of God. Among human beings, who knows what pertains to a person except the spirit of the person that is within? Similarly, no one knows what pertains to God except the Spirit of God." (1 Cor 2:10–11)

To go back to the example of a longtime married couple: Spouses get to know each other most intimately over the course of many years. They get to know each other intuitively, beyond words. It is enough to simply sit in one another's presence and be close to each other, beyond mere words or emotional highs or lows. It is one of the blessings of traditional marriage. But no matter how well a man knows his wife, she will always remain a mystery to him. (I also joke that she probably had him figured out on the first date.)

And the fact is that most of us really do not know ourselves either. Let's be honest—how many of us wake up some days wondering who is looking back at us in the mirror? Some of us say with astonishment, "Who is that old guy [or gal]?" Many days we just don't seem to be "in our own skin." We don't understand ourselves, much less why we do the things we don't want to do, and don't do the things we want to do. This is because we do not know who we really were created to be by God, and we have usually settled for a version of ourselves that falls far short of that beautiful reality. (We will return to this later in this book when treating the spirit, soul, and body in the human person.)

Only God can know us fully, for only God is closer to us than we are to ourselves. Therefore, real mercy can only be found in God, and we can only be merciful to others insofar as we know God. When we ask for mercy we are literally calling out for God to fill us up with the Spirit so that we might become who we were really created to be.

But we cannot be filled until we are empty of the old, incomplete self. You know that self. It's the one that does not make us happy, and probably doesn't make others very happy either. We hang on to it as if our life depended on it. But that self is dragging us down. It is keeping us from being happy, content, and blessed. And it is keeping us from being a blessing to others. We must let go of that old self through the daily cross of Christ. Only then can we be born again every day in Jesus and be the full human being we were created to be.

This can be really scary. If we let go, who will be left? But God loves us more than we love ourselves, so we can trust. It is like falling backward into the arms of trusted friends. It is scary, but they will catch us. If mere human friends can be counted on to catch us, how much more can we count on God to catch us? Not only does he catch us, but he also reveals who we will really be raised back up to be in Christ. And that version of ourselves will always be much better than the self we have settled for so far in our life.

And with the Jesus Prayer it is as easy as breathing! Breathe in the fullness of Jesus, and breathe out anything standing between you and Jesus. It sounds so simple, and it is. But it takes a lifetime to really grow into the depths of the mercy of God through Jesus Christ. So breathe in. Then breathe out, and ask for the fullness of mercy. It is asking a lot. But God will answer that heartfelt prayer through Jesus if we dare to make our next breath a genuine prayer. Are you experiencing that mercy yet?

8 : ON ME

As Catholics, we hear it all the time: "a personal love relationship with Jesus Christ." We sometimes joke about the phrase regarding our Evangelical brothers and sisters. But recent popes have also emphasized the necessity for a love relationship with Jesus that is personal. On January 13, 2013, Catholic News Service reported that during a baptism Pope Benedict "told the parents that their children's baptism would bring them into a 'personal relationship with Jesus' that would give their lives meaning: 'Only in this friendship is the great potential of the human condition truly revealed and we can experience what is beautiful and what is free.'" Pope Francis is also starting his pontificate with a clear emphasis on a love relationship with Jesus Christ as the basis for our Catholic Christian faith.

Since the time of Pope John Paul II Catholics have shifted from describing the Church as the "body of Christ" to describing it as the "people of God" and "*communio,*" or "communion." *Communion* simply means "common union." It is about a union with Jesus that is both private and communal. Both are personal.

When I first became a Catholic, I was greatly attracted to the more communal aspect of Catholic spirituality and life. We are a de facto community in humanity. As John Donne wrote in poetry and Thomas Merton echoed in the title of his book,

"No Man Is An Island." Humanity is communal, or tribal, from its beginnings. We are not isolated from creation or from each other. When we are called to unite with God, we do so personally, but we do so in the context of the community of faith, humanity, and creation. It is simply unavoidable. As St. Paul says, "But how can they call on him in whom they have not believed? And how can they believe in him of whom they have not heard? And how can they hear without someone to preach? And how can people preach unless they are sent?" (Rom 10:14–15) Even St. Paul, who received his commission from Jesus directly, had to go to discern that calling with those who actually walked with Christ on earth. (Gal 2:1–10) We cannot even proclaim Christ without the help of community in some form. There must be someone to send, someone to receive, and someone to discern and confirm.

When I first came into the Catholic Church I loved (and still love) the rich monastic and Franciscan tradition that emphasizes both personal relationship with God through Jesus and the communal context of that relationship. Even hermits found strength by grouping together into loose-knit, but very real, colonies that supported one another in the solitude and in weekly prayer, fellowship, and Eucharist, not to mention the ongoing conferences given by the fathers and mothers. The fact that there still exists support for those who want to get radical but not fanatical in following Jesus speaks volumes.

But this communal context does not exclude the very real need for a personal response to the call of Jesus. Jesus says, "Behold, I stand at the door and knock. If anyone hears my voice and opens the door, [then] I will enter his house and dine with him, and he with me." (Rv 3:20) I love the painting of this scene, in which there is no doorknob on Jesus's side, but only on ours. The response to his call to open the door is personal, and only we can open it.

I often laugh with the married men of a congregation that Catholics are so communal that we guys think that when our wife goes to Mass, it also counts for us. But it doesn't work that way. No one else can decide to respond to the call of Jesus for us. As St. Paul writes to the Galatians, "Bear one another's burdens [Greek βαροσ (*baros*)], and so fulfill the law of Christ." (Gal 6:2) But just a few verses down he says that everyone must bear their own burden (Greek φορτιον [*phortion*]; Gal 6:5). These are two different words for "burden," and the latter is translated as "load" in most modern versions. Both mean "weight" in one capacity or another, so the point is the same. We can bear one another's burdens through prayer and acts of mercy, but regarding salvation itself each of us must make our own personal decision to follow Jesus. No one can make that decision for us.

It is symbolized in church. We are baptized personally, but in the context of a community. We hear the Word of God proclaimed in a community worship experience, and Scriptures can be explained and expounded. But no one can take them into our life for us. We must listen and respond personally. We receive the Eucharist personally. No one can do it for us. But it is in the context of community. Our experience in the local parish is a symbol of this balance of personal relationship and community. It is personal, intimate, and private, yet it is also communal.

The same is true of Jesus himself. His birth was into a family in the human and faith family, but it was personal. It was intimate. No one could do it for him. His reaching out to minister to crowds and each individual was personal. No one could do it for him. His faith to step out as a man and do the work of his father despite the apparent limitations of the world was personal. It took courage and faith. It took guts. No one could do it for him. His death on the cross was painful and personal. It was a communal humiliation, but he was totally alone on that cross. The pain was real and it was terribly personal. No one could do it for him. And last but not least, the glory of his Resurrection was witnessed by hundreds; it was communal. But it was personal. No one could rise up and go forth from that tomb for him. He had to rise up and walk. No one could do it for him.

So the question is: Will you and I respond to the call from Christ? We can encourage each other in community. But no one can do it for us. We must respond personally. Will you and I follow Jesus today? That is the challenge of the seemingly obvious and simple words *on me*. It is personal. No one can do it for us. Will you and I respond personally to the call of Jesus?

9: A SINNER

Sin is a most misunderstood concept today. Some emphasize it too much and become negative and weird. Some deny it altogether and also become weird. We live in a world where the secular humanist idea has been to throw the concept of sin based on divine revelation out altogether and just call holy that which the majority agrees to. Conversely, believers sometimes react by getting obsessive about sin. Neither really works. A healthy balance is needed.

Most religions believe in some notion of what we call sin. The train has a wheel or two of the track, or we wouldn't need religious or moral teaching at all. We would all just "get it" on our own. But we don't, so we need the help of established teachers and religious guides. Sin is real. And it is deadly if left unaddressed. The wheels off the track of our spiritual and moral life create a constant drag on our spiritual progress, and can even derail the train and cause injury and death.

Of course, all who know even a bit of Scripture know this famous passage: "all have sinned and are deprived of the glory of God. They are justified freely by his grace through the redemption in Christ Jesus." (Rom 3:23–24) They might also know, "For the wages of sin is death, but the gift of God is eternal life in Christ Jesus our Lord." (Rom 6:23) We ask why: Why does sin bring forth death? How does this happen? Scripture describes the process in a way that sheds some light on the matter. "Rather, each person is tempted when he is lured and enticed by his own desire. Then desire conceives and brings forth sin, and when sin reaches maturity it gives birth to death." (Jas 1:14–15) It is a process that requires human cooperation.

The word *sin* primarily comes from the Greek αμαρτια (*hamartia*), and it means "to miss the mark." It was used of getting off the path on a journey, to err or be mistaken. It was also used in archery tournaments when the arrow missed the bull's-eye. Usually the archers hit the target but miss the perfect bull's-eye.

We are like those archers. We are created in the image of God, so we long for goodness, truth, beauty, love, justice, and so on. We want good things. But sometimes we do not realize God is the creator of good, and the highest good. Therefore we miss the perfect center and balance of the target in the bull's-eye. We miss perfection. This doesn't seem so bad. But we are told that sin brings forth death. What does that mean?

Think of a tire on a car. I spend a lot of time driving around the United States in our ministry vans or buses. I have learned to "feel" the car, the wheel, and the tires as they turn one mile after mile of highway. When the tires are out of balance it can cause trouble. First it just creates a little shimmy or vibration. Left uncorrected it can cause a vibration that begins to really shake the car. If still left unfixed it can cause an accident that can result in death on the highway.

That's basically what sin is like. We are traveling down a spiritual highway throughout our lifetime. We are usually headed in the right direction. But sometimes we develop an imbalance, or sin, as we travel. We might miss the mark and hit a pothole that throws the wheels and tires out of balance. If it isn't corrected, it can eventually cause death. The death might be spiritual instead of physical, but it is real.

Sin also has a process. The early monastic fathers and mothers learned about this in their "laboratories" and teach it in some detail. St. Augustine reduced a rather long description into three easy-to-understand steps. First there is temptation. Second, there is "entertaining" sin in the mind and feelings. Third, there is action. We are not responsible for the first stage. That happens to everyone. Even Jesus was tempted, in every way we are, but he never gave in to the temptation to sin. "For we do not have a high priest who is unable to sympathize with our weaknesses, but one who in every respect has been tempted as we are, yet without sin." (Heb 4:15) Jesus was tempted, but he did not entertain tempting thoughts, emotions, and sensual impulses, which we usually call "lust."

The fathers and mothers tell us that devils (real, willful, spiritual, usually disembodied entities) can fill the mind with tempting thoughts and can even stimulate the body. But they cannot make us sin. That is something only we can do. It is personal. And it is a matter of the will. The will is the faculty of decision that directs thoughts and emotions. It is neither cold thought nor heated emotion. It is a balance of the two, like a wagon driver who directs two horses skillfully. We must choose to resist, and avail ourselves of the grace of God to empower us to overcome the sin. As St. James writes, "So submit yourselves to God. Resist the devil, and he will flee from you. Draw near to God, and he will draw near to you." (Jas 4:7–8) This is serious stuff, a matter of life and death.

Now let's lighten it up a bit. But this remains important. There are two paradigms for what sin is like that are worth mentioning here. One is from apocryphal Lutheran tradition. The other is from St. Bonaventure.

The first says that sin is like a pile of dung covered with snow. Sin is serious, so it is described as turning the human soul to a pile of dung. It is extreme, as in Isaiah 64, which says that because of sin, "We have all become like something unclean, all our just deeds are like polluted rags." (Is 64:5) The atonement and forgiveness of Jesus is like a thin layer of snow that covers the pile of dung. When God the Father looks down from heaven he does not see the pile of dung; instead he sees a beautiful, lily white pile of snow. Isaiah also says, "Come now, let us set things right, says the Lord: Though your sins be like scarlet, they may become white as snow." (Is 1:18) But all you have to do is kick this lily white pile of snow, and whew! It lets up a stink and reveals its true nature.

The problem with this analogy is that ultimately, even after the redemption that cost Jesus his life, we remain a pile of dung. This traps us in an essential self-image that is imbalanced and unhealthy. And when we feel this way about ourselves, we begin to project that same image onto everyone else in our life. No matter how well a person may do, even in Christ, we essentially think that he or she is just a pile of dung. This image dehumanizes others and ourselves. In the final analysis it simply does not work.

St. Bonaventure uses an analogy that is healthier and far more positive, without losing the deadly nature of sin. He says that the human soul is like a mirror created to reflect the beautiful image and likeness of God. Sin is like dust and dirt that can collect on the mirror. At first it dulls the image, then it begins to obscure parts of it. If left uncleansed it can obscure the image altogether. But the good news is: Jesus does windows!

Yes, Jesus can cleanse the mirror so that we might reflect the beautiful image and likeness of God again. All through our spiritual life this cleansing must be repeated through confession and repentance.

This is a more healthy and balanced analogy. No matter how badly we sin, the potential to reflect the image and likeness of God remains deep within us. There is no sinner in the entire world, no matter how badly he or she has sinned, who cannot be forgiven by Jesus and empowered by the Spirit to avoid the sin in the future. This radically affects our self-image and our essential image of others. Never can we treat ourselves as a pile of dung or a disposable thing due to sin. Never again can we treat people as mere things that we use, even in working out our salvation. Instead, we all remain "mirrors" created to reflect the beautiful, the living image and likeness of God.

But there is one other word for "sin" worth mentioning here. The other Greek word is σκανδαλιζω (*skandalizo*), and it means "scandal." Jesus literally becomes a scandal so that we might be saved (the "offense" of Rom 9:32). This is utterly costly for Jesus, and completely personal. How can we not take his great gift of love sacrifice for us seriously when it cost him so much? He literally became sin; he became scandal for us so that we might be completely redeemed and saved from our own scandal of sin.

So sin is serious, but it is not as bad as what some think. It is deadly, but it does not reduce all of creation to death after Jesus Christ. Creation is redeemed, and so are we, as well as anyone who sincerely follows God. This is all possible through Jesus. It is good news. It transforms our sin into righteousness and our death into new life. See, there it is again: Nothing is impossible with God!

10: CONCLUSION

Now that we have looked at the specific meanings of the words of the Jesus Prayer, we must actually pray it. We do that by breathing in and breathing out with the words of the prayer. We do not get sidetracked into obsessing about the words, but we do intuit the prayer with our spirit in the Spirit as we pray. Knowing the meaning of the words adds depth to our intuition. But getting sidetracked and focusing on the intellectual meaning alone will keep us from sinking deeper into the spiritual realities of the prayer. So the meaning of the words is very important, but it is not the final goal of the prayer. The goal remains simple communion with Jesus and the people of God in the Church that spans space and time.

So let's try it. Breathe in: "Lord Jesus Christ, Son of God." Breathe out: "Have mercy on me, a sinner." Now repeat it. Once more. Now get into the rhythm of the prayer by praying it for a few minutes. As you do this you will sense Jesus filling you through the Spirit. You'll feel a simple letting go of all that stands between you and a full communion with Jesus and the Church. It will happen almost naturally with each repeating breath.

One thing you will notice is that the prayer will slow down to the rhythm of your breathing, and become a living part of you. You will begin to enter into the reality of St. Francis, who sought "not so much to pray, but to become a prayer." The prayer will slowly transform your whole life.

This is simple, but it is not simplistic. And it is not always easy. It takes a lifetime. And it takes faith-filled courage. Like peeling an onion, layer by layer, Jesus will reveal and strip back everything that still separates us from a full communion. This can be painful, so it takes courage. But if we have the faith to see it through we will discover that our life is being changed, and changed for the better in Jesus Christ and the Church.

This practice of breathing a prayer can be applied to all our personal devotions and prayers. It works for the Marian Rosary as well as the Jesus Prayer.

Breathe in: Hail Mary, full of grace, the Lord is with you.

Breathe out: Blessed are you among women. And blessed is the fruit of your womb, Jesus.

Breathe in: Holy Mary, Mother of God

Breathe out: Pray for us sinners, now, and at the hour of our death.

This can also be applied to private prayers. With *lectio divina*, or sacred reading, we can take a few moments to simply breathe in Jesus and breathe out all that is standing between him and us before we pray the Scriptures or other sacred writings. Keeping the breath slowed to a comfortable pace, we read. After reading we can let the words of the scriptural passage soak in as we breathe and pray in the breath, or Spirit of God.

The real key to private devotion of any kind is this: Before the Church or the world can be renewed in Christ, we must be renewed in Christ. Before the Church or nations change, people must change. If we want the Church to get better, we must get better. If we want to change the world, we must first change our own life.

This is the ministry we are taking all across America and to other parts of the world. We are renewing the Church one parish at a time, and the people of God one human heart at a time. That is where private prayer and devotion fits into the renewal of the greater Church and world. Great things start small. Community changes for the better when people change for the better. Then the community helps keep that renewal alive.

As we take this ministry all around the world folks are saying that this little section on the Jesus Prayer truly transforms their personal prayer life. It really works! I suggest taking twenty minutes a day, twice a day if possible. Out of twenty minutes you will get about two minutes of deep, contemplative prayer. The rest will be settling in, and gently coming out. And that will be enough to face any challenge the world can send our way.

You will notice a pattern of progress as well. After a few days you will see some change for the better, then again after a few months, and then after a few years. After about ten years you will see a huge change that will not easily be taken from you. Many say, "But I'm too old. I don't have ten years!" That might be true. But none of us really knows how much time we have left. It could be years, days, or even hours. So start right now. Use the time we have well. As the country song says, "Live every day like you're dying." And live every day like you will be here for many, many more years. Then we will live every day to the fullest in Christ.

In the next section we will look at the communal prayer for the Orthodox Catholic Church—the Divine Liturgy, the Eucharist, or what we simply call the Mass. It is my favorite part of this ministry and of my spiritual life. So I invite you to take a few moments, hours, or even a day to absorb what we have already covered before moving on to the more corporate part of our life in Christ in the Church.

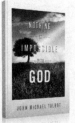

PART III:
Walk Through the Liturgy

Now we move to the most important part of this book, the walk through the Liturgy. The Liturgy is often called the "source and summit" of our Christian life. I agree.

But I also recognize that most folks tend to sleepwalk through the average Mass at the local parish, which is a shame. We have the greatest treasure on earth, and we neither fully experience it nor share it effectively with others. No wonder our non-Catholic brothers and sisters sometimes call the Mass "the dance of the dead." I might take some offense at this title, for I certainly know many lively Catholic Christians who find great life in the Mass. But I cannot help but notice that many in the pews in parishes across the country seem to be asleep at the wheel. And if we don't correct this we could end up crashing, and killing many innocent folks.

At the beginning of this book I mentioned that only seventeen percent of Catholics and fifteen percent of Catholic youth actually attend Mass on Sunday. And most of these are obviously unengaged and just mumbling and shuffling their way through the Liturgy. They are certainly not actively engaged. Is it any wonder that fifty percent of the megachurches down the street are filled with nonpracticing Catholics who not only go there, but go with unbridled enthusiasm? Not only do they go to the megachurch, but they can't wait to get there, and they don't want to leave when the service is over. Why?

I think it comes down to two things: music and preaching. Megachurches have great music that fully engages the congregation, and they have motivational preaching and teaching. We Catholics usually have a few parishes in each diocese that are really great faith communities, but despite the protestations of many, we pretty consistently fail in these two areas. The sad thing is that we are often clueless about the fact that we are missing the mark, and we are defensive about the success of the megachurches. Why? We tend to be a fairly ingrown culture. So we walk around telling ourselves how great we are doing, when the rest of the world knows how badly we are failing. It is the proverbial case of the emperor's new clothes: Everyone knows, but no one will admit it and actually speak out.

But we don't have to settle for this self-delusion. There are simple things that we can do to fix this once we admit that we have a problem and are willing to do something about it. But it takes the full cooperation of both the congregation and the pastoral staff of the parish, most especially the senior pastor.

Let's take some steps now to do something about it.

In this treatment we are going to walk through the Liturgy, body, soul, and spirit. The body will be symbolized by the narthex and nave, the soul will be symbolized by the ambo, and the altar in the sanctuary will symbolize the spirit.

Let's get started!

11: LITURGY

Let's begin with the basics. What does *liturgy* mean? When I ask this question at parish missions folks answer with a variety of things. They might say it means worship, praise, prayer, or even service. Good as they are, none of these is really correct. Sooner or later someone will call out, "the work of the people!" That is the correct answer.

The word *liturgy* comes from the Greek λειτουργία or λητουργία (*leitourgia*), and it simply means "the work of the people." It comes from λαός (*Laos*), meaning "the people," and the root ἔργο (*ergon*), meaning "work." It could apply to public works like road or bridge building, or, God help us, even political public service! But it also was used to describe the people's part in pagan worship, so Christians co-opted the word.

The concept of liturgy is taken for granted, though the word is not directly found in the Scriptures, but translated as ministry, worship, service, or offering and collection. But liturgy was a common reality in worship in the time of Christ. Today it can be widely applied to any church or faith community that uses an order of worship. Think about it. Even in nonliturgical churches and communities a certain pattern of worship emerges. Usually it amounts to some songs of worship and praise, reading Scriptures, preaching, intercessions, and some sacramental celebration that occurs either weekly or from time to time.

Guess what? That's a liturgy! So even so-called nonliturgical churches are liturgical, whether they want to be or not.

The same is true of ritual. Ritual makes our life appropriately predictable, and more civilized. When you walk up to meet someone in our culture you usually say, "Hello, my name is so and so," and shake his or her hand. It is a ritual that makes meeting someone new more comfortable, which makes it easier to forge deeper relationships from there. The problem arises when we get stuck in the ritual and never go on into deeper relationships with some of the many you ordinarily meet in the course of daily life. In fact, a life without ritual is filled with uncertainty, and can even lapse into chaos. In that sense, a life without ritual becomes uncivilized. So ritual isn't bad; it is good. But it must be used correctly.

But *liturgy* also has another meaning, which is even more challenging. In the fifth century St. Benedict, the father of Western monasticism, called what we now call the "Liturgy of the Hours" the "work of God." Wow, the work of God! That means that in *liturgy* the work of the people comes together with the work of God. Literally, in liturgy heaven and earth meet; God and humanity are joined. It is not simply the repetition of a set of words that we are required to memorize or read in order to do our part. It is not just about getting the words right. It is where heaven and earth come together.

Every word, every gesture, and every sacrament are where God and humanity, heaven and earth, meet. This supernaturalizes the entire process of liturgical worship, or the celebration of the Liturgy. God is truly present in every Liturgy. He is not being talked about; he is actually right there with us. We are already in heaven during every Liturgy.

So we are going to take a walk through the Liturgy, using body, soul, and spirit. Let's begin the walk. But let's not take it for granted or sleepwalk through it. We are walking on holy ground.

12: BODY, SOUL, AND SPIRIT

We are going to walk through the Liturgy from body to soul to spirit. We will enter into the parish church through the narthex, or the place for the congregation with our body. We will journey into the sanctuary to the ambo, from which the Scriptures are proclaimed, and the homily is preached with the soul. We will conclude our journey by moving into the sanctuary to the altar of the Eucharist with the Spirit. The journey will be complete, involving and awakening every aspect of our human being with the greatest gift from God through Jesus in the Eucharist at every Mass.

In this paradigm we will follow classical stages of prayer, meditation, and contemplation from the Christian tradition. The body includes the senses, chemical emotions, and neurological thoughts. The soul is the spiritual reason, or spiritual mind. And the spirit is the contemplative intuition. The body is the place for asceticism and discipline. The soul is the place for meditation that includes the use of mental images and imagination. And the spirit is the place for pure contemplation beyond images, names, or form.

Where do we get that description of our being? It comes from St. Paul's First Letter to the Thessalonians. He says, "May the God of peace himself make you perfectly holy and may you entirely, spirit, soul, and body, be preserved blameless for the coming of our Lord Jesus Christ." (1 Thes 5:23)

This is not really a strict or scientific anthropology, but it is a good place to start, and it will serve our purposes for this liturgical walk. Jesus also speaks of a twofold description of body and soul: "And do not be afraid of those who kill the body but cannot kill the soul; rather, be afraid of the one who can destroy both soul and body in Gehenna." (Mt 10:28) So we do not want to be too literal in our understanding of the spiritual and physical parts that make up the human being, but they are helpful. Plus, these parts cannot be strictly separated. The human being remains an integrated whole. It is impossible to completely separate one part from the other. It requires all three—body, soul, and spirit—working in concert to make us fully human.

Having said that, what are these three biblical things that make us human? Let's take a deeper look at each one.

BODY

The biblical Greek word for "body" is σωμα (*soma*), meaning "the physical part of what we are." It can also refer to that which "casts a shadow." Pretty cool, but nothing terribly revelatory.

The body is mainly just what we think it is: the sensual part of us. We sometimes speak of the five senses: sight, hearing, taste, touch, and smell. No great mystery there. But it also includes much, much more.

Modern science would tell us that the emotions are largely chemical. For instance, we know that when our chemistry is out of balance we sometimes get emotionally unstable. This imbalance can cause conditions from low blood sugar to bipolar disorder. Probably the greatest proof of this is that we have not only psychology but also psychiatry. Psychology is mainly professional counseling. Psychiatry includes not only counseling but also medication. Medication helps balance our chemical self so that counseling will actually work. Have any of you felt your chemistry out of whack and found it difficult to think clearly? Sure you have, and so have I. So part of our emotional self is physical; it is part of the body.

But our body also includes our brain chemistry, or our neurology. The brain is made up of millions of electrical impulses that interact with the chemistry and brain cells. It is physical. So thoughts are partly physical; they are part of the body.

This has some very cool ramifications. How many of us struggle with negative thoughts? I hope your hand is up, for I know mine is! Part of that is very physical, so if we think negatively, we're more likely to do so the next time we face a challenge and a choice. It becomes a matter of habit.

Scripture says that we are what we think (Prv 23:7 NKJV). "Finally, brothers, whatever is true, whatever is honorable, whatever is just, whatever is pure, whatever is lovely, whatever is gracious, if there is any excellence and if there is anything worthy of praise, think about these things." (Phil 4:8) "We have the mind of Christ." (1 Cor 2:16) If you habitually think it, most likely you will do or say it. As we say, "Garbage in, garbage out." If we fill the mind with the negative and coarse things of the world, we will become like those things. If we fill our minds with the beautiful and wonderful things of God, we will become like the beautiful and wonderful things of God.

The way out? Choose. Make a decision to think positively. Positive thoughts overcome negative thoughts; it is a matter of the will. It isn't always easy at first. But the more we do it, the easier it gets. As Thomas à Kempis said in *The Imitation of Christ*, good habit overcomes bad habit.

SOUL

The primary biblical Greek word for "soul" is ψυχη (*psyche*), meaning "the rational part of our spiritual self," or "breath." It literally means "air, wind, and breath." It is the spiritual reason that drives the mere physical function of thought. It is the spirit thought that drives and complements our brain thought.

Now, there are many words for "mind" and "thought" in Greek, and they can overlap. They can also be confusing for a typical Westerner looking into the Greek usage.

διανοια (*dianoia*) means "inner imagination"; it is used in the famous passage, "You shall love the Lord, your God, with all your heart, with all your soul, and with all your mind. " (Mt 22:37)

φρονεω (*phroneo*) refers to a kind of sentiment or opinion, and it is used in "Get behind me, Satan! You are an obstacle to me. You are thinking not as God does, but as human beings do." (Mt 16:23)

νουσ (*nous*) means "discerning faculty." St. Paul would say, "For I take delight in the law of God, in my inner self, but I see in my members another principle at war with the law of my mind, taking me captive to the law of sin that dwells in my members." (Rom 7:22–23) The Greek monastics sometimes call the *nous* the most spiritual part of the human person.

For our purposes I would like to jump ahead a bit to St. Bonaventure in the thirteenth and fourteenth centuries. He is sometimes called the second founder of the Franciscan Order, because he saved the order from disintegrating into division and falling apart. He was also respected by Eastern Christians, and once made into a cardinal archbishop was sent by Rome to try to reestablish unity between the Christian East and West.

St. Bonaventure wrote a wonderful spiritual treatise called the Itinerarium Mentis ad Deum. When translated it is sometimes called The Journey of the Soul to God, and sometimes The Journey of the Mind to God. Using Bonaventure we can call the soul the "spiritual mind," or the part of the human being that is spiritual reason. Interestingly, the Greek word for "soul," or "psyche," is also the root word for "psychology."

So we can call the soul the "spiritual mind." It is deeper than mere brain thought, and it includes the thoughts of the spiritual mind.

SPIRIT

Recall that the biblical Greek word for "spirit" is πνευμα (*pneuma*), meaning "air, wind, and breath." It also means the "rational" part of the soul. Some Greek monastics would call the *nous* the spirit. So what's the difference between spirit and soul? I dunno!

When we merely use the etymology of words it is indeed difficult to separate the spirit from the soul. Perhaps that is precisely why the book of Hebrews says, "Indeed, the word of God is living and effective, sharper than any two-edged sword, penetrating even between soul and spirit, joints and marrow, and able to discern reflections and thoughts of the heart." (Heb 4:12) The implication is that with mere human reason it is very difficult to tell the difference.

Along with spirituality, modern psychology and even parapsychology give us some help here. I would like to speak of the spirit as the place of pure spiritual intuition. It builds on the senses, emotions, and thoughts of the body and soul, but surpasses them all.

What is intuition? It is that part of our humanity that looks at the sunrise or sunset and simply says, "ahh," in order to deeply understand it. It is a knowing beyond mere intellectual, emotional, or sensual knowing. It is the knowing beyond knowledge.

I am reminded of a cartoon of two Franciscan friars known for their love of creation, contemplating a sunrise. One says to the other, "Notice his use of color here!" Wonderful as this appreciation is, it is not pure intuition. It is still knowing on the level of body and soul. Intuition would simply look on in profound silence that understands on the level of the spirit and speaks even more than words. It is the place of pure contemplation.

We have all had that contemplative experience. Whenever we spend time with a loved one or friend and break through into rich and wonderful silence that is somehow beyond the time and space of the body or soul, we experience it. In such moments in space and time we break through to eternity and infinity—for example, when we look at a flower, tree, or creation and experience the Creator beyond words. We experience it when we listen to a piece of music and somehow break through to eternity. These are breakthroughs into what we call "contemplation." They are flashes of intuition that break though to the eternal in an instant.

The monastics and mystics of the Christian East say that the human spirit has the capacity for the eternal and the infinite. The spirit can experience eternity in the now, and infinity while being in the finite world. In other words, we can be everywhere at once, and in eternity in a flash. We can be in the past, present, and future for eternity all at once. Wow! This all happens though our participation in Christ. St. Paul says profoundly that God has "raised us up with him, and seated us with him in the heavens in Christ Jesus, that in the ages to come he might show the immeasurable riches of his grace in his kindness to us in Christ Jesus." (Eph 2:6–7) In other words, we are already in eternity and infinity in Jesus Christ.

Now, I don't know about you, but my body is not in eternity! It is sitting in a chair in a hotel while on a ministry trip writing this chapter. It is often bouncing from town to town in parishes throughout Middle America. In such places my emotions are certainly rarely in eternity. They are very much conditioned by what is happening all around me in space and time. I'm refreshed or tired, filled or hungry, healthy or sick. My thoughts process the senses, and my emotions follow. It is so immediate that it seems impossible to understand, but it is a process that is most real.

My thoughts might be able to remember the past and to hope for the future, but even they cannot break though entirely into eternity and infinity. St. Paul says, "What eye has not seen, and ear has not heard, and what has not entered the human heart [or "what no human mind has conceived" (NIV Bible)], what God has prepared for those who love him, this God has revealed to us through the Spirit. For the Spirit scrutinizes everything, even the depths of God." (1 Cor 2:9–10) In other words, it has not even dawned on our heart or mind. We haven't even imagined it yet. But these things can be grasped through the intuitions of the spirit. This is especially true when we are aided by the Holy Spirit of God.

The Eastern Christian fathers say that the human spirit has the capacity for the eternal and the infinite. Therefore, it can be in the past, the present, and the future all at once. Wow! That is nothing short of stunning. But it is the primary intuitive and contemplative state of the human being that operates with the spirit first.

SIN

Now, if I were to ask you what these three things were, you would probably not say the more biblical spirit, soul, and body. You would probably say body, soul, and spirit. Why? Because we are sinners, and have gotten things turned upside down.

The reality is that most of us get stuck in the senses, emotions, and thoughts of the body and soul, and rarely break through to the spirit. We have settled for a version of ourselves that is incomplete at best, and doesn't make us or anyone else genuinely happy. How does it work?

Most of us first get stuck in the senses. As soon as we sense something we think it. Then our emotions react according to the pleasure or discomfort of the sensual experience. Forgotten, the spirit gets buried, and it dies. But it doesn't stop there. It changes our whole identity.

The problem is that once we settle for this incomplete identity we tend to operate that way in other things, in all the areas of our life. Once we forget the spirit and start operating without it, we tend to think that we are only body and soul, or senses, thoughts, and emotions. Then we become very defensive if someone doesn't agree with our ideas or opinions. This even invades religion. Soon we no longer have doctrines to explain our spiritual experience, but we replace doctrine with spiritual experience. Our religion shifts from knowing God to knowing *about* God. There is a vast difference. And we remain essentially unfulfilled in the process. Religions are filled with folks who have settled for that incomplete identity and version of faith. It is a world turned upside down.

It is not so much that the faculties we have settled for are wrong, but they are out of place, and cannot be what they were created by God to be. We all have senses, emotions, and thoughts. But they are supposed to serve the spirit. Instead we have ignored spirit and focused on the servants. Therefore we all end up enslaved.

SALVATION

How do we get out of this upside-down world? How do we become complete? How do we get the servants to serve instead of running roughshod and ruling over the deepest part of who we are, the spirit? We must completely let go of the old and incomplete self through the cross of Christ. The old, incomplete self must die through the death of Jesus Christ. Only then can the spirit be born again in the Spirit through the Resurrection of Jesus Christ. The answer is simple: the cross and Resurrection of Jesus. He does not merely point the way; he *is* the way, truth, and life.

When we die to the old, disordered self of senses, thoughts, and emotions, then the spirit is born again in the Spirit; the spirit takes the lead again. The thoughts can fulfill their rightful place to facilitate the spirit. The emotions can empower us to godly enthusiasm. And the senses can become the bodily vehicle from which this wonderful mystery can unfold in the phenomenal world. Everything is put in its right place, and everything can prosper by doing the job it was created to do. Then we are truly blessed, as Jesus promised in the Beatitudes.

This means that we walk with a constant intuition of eternity and infinity as our primary state of being. We seek not so much to pray, but to become a prayer. We walk in an intuition of contemplation. The mind, emotions, and senses facilitate us in this state according to their gift and capacity. But they are not primary. They have found their rightful place, and prosper by facilitating the complete human being to be what and who we were originally created to be, and who we have now been redeemed to be once more in Christ.

In the Liturgy, or the Mass, God meets us right where we are. Like the father leaving the security of the house to meet his son with the first signs of repentance in the parable of the prodigal son (Lk 17:11–32), God meets us through the senses, thoughts, and emotions of the body, and brings us into the spiritual mind of the soul. Finally, he ushers us into the "holy of holies," in the Eucharist at the altar.

Through the Liturgy, through the Mass, we are met where we are in order for God to lead us back to where we were originally intended to be through Jesus Christ. The Mass is the special sacramental way that Jesus gave the Church to lead us back to God. It is precious. It is a pearl of great price. Unfortunately, we so often treat it like an old set of work clothes. It is time to rediscover the treasure of the Mass as the special gift of Jesus to lead us back to the right priorities of God.

So let's begin our walk through the Liturgy, body, soul, and spirit. Let's be born again in Jesus Christ!

13: BODY

We begin our walk through the Liturgy with the body. Why? Because we are sinners. God is merciful, so he meets us right where we are. Most of us are still stuck in the senses of the body. "I'm too hot, too cold, hungry, thirsty, tired, sick," and so on are all-too-common cries that we hear. So, like the father in the parable of the prodigal son, God leaves the security of heaven to meet us right where we are. He meets us in the senses of the body.

BODY: COME TO CHURCH AND "BROTHER ASS"

The first thing about meeting us in the body during the Liturgy is so obvious that we often overlook it: We have to bring the body to church! We have to get out of bed, get dressed, and go to church in order to participate in the Liturgy.

St. Francis of Assisi called his body Brother Ass. He wasn't talking about his backside, but about the donkey. When Jesus rides into Jerusalem on Palm Sunday, Scripture says, "Behold, your king comes to you, meek and riding on an ass, and on a colt, the foal of a beast of burden." (Mt 21:5) Why is the body called an "ass," or "donkey"? Because it tends not to do what you want it to do. If you want it to go, it resists. If you want it to stop, it wants to keep on going.

We all experience this in some way or another. When it's time to go to church we may have all kinds of reasons why we could stay at home. We have all kinds of things that we are already doing that we don't want to interrupt. Some of this is secular, and some is religious. Of course, some want to stay home and rest on a day off from work. Some want to get the noon meal ready. Some want to get ready for the football game. Kids often want to get ready for the soccer game later in the day.

We can also have religious reasons. Perhaps we are engaged in private prayer or Bible study. We might not want to interrupt it to go to a Mass that is mediocre at best. Shouldn't we stay in private prayer or sacred study of the Scriptures of the day, or patristics, or Church teaching instead of going to the parish to hear a rather typical non-motivational homily? These are common excuses.

This touches on the "I'm spiritual, but not religious" mentality so often heard in today's individualistic culture. More and more people are saying that they might believe in God or Jesus, but they no longer believe in the Church or even feel the need to worship with others in any organized religious setting at all.

It is true that religion without spirituality is lifeless and dead. But conversely spirituality without religion is non-incarnate and fluffy, with no real feet on the ground. Jesus was spirit, soul, and body. He was the Word incarnate. Likewise the early Church believed in both the mystical and organizational aspects of the Church. It is like a dove: You need two wings to really fly. One wing is religion, and the other is spirituality. Many folks try to fly with only one wing. It simply doesn't work! You need both spirituality and religion in order for the dove of God to fly.

It is only by dragging Brother Ass to church that we will get the fullness of the grace God offers to us during each Mass. We might want to stay home, or we might believe that we pray better at home. But even monks go to the monastic church to celebrate the Liturgy. Likewise, we must get ourselves to the local parish church in order to receive the full benefit of the Mass, the "source and summit" of our life in Christ as a united people.

SIGN OF THE CROSS: DIE TO THE OLD SELF AND RISE UP A NEW CREATION IN CHRIST

The first thing we do when we enter a Catholic Church is stunning: We dip our hand in holy water and make the sign of the cross. This is a powerful symbol that is often overlooked, or done rather routinely without really understanding what we are doing.

We place holy water at the doorway of our parish churches. It is a symbol of our baptism and the dying of the person we were through the cross of Jesus, and the rising up of a new creation through his Resurrection. This is traceable back to the blood placed on the doorposts of the Jewish people during the first Passover, before their exodus from Egypt:

Go and procure lambs for your families, and slaughter the Passover victims. Then take a bunch of hyssop, and dipping it in the blood that is in the basin, apply some of this blood to the lintel and the two doorposts. And none of you shall go outdoors until morning. For when the Lord goes by to strike down the Egyptians, seeing the blood on the lintel and the two doorposts, the Lord will pass over that door and not let the destroyer come into your houses to strike you down. (Ex 12:21–23)

To this day Orthodox Jewish believers place a scroll on the doorpost, and touch it prayerfully whenever they enter or leave their houses. Christians continue this by placing the waters of baptism in holy water, and baptismal fonts at the entrance of our parish church buildings. Nowadays our full-immersion Catholic baptismal fonts are so beautiful that they have become the envy of some of my Baptist pastor buddies!

This emphasizes the real reason we come to church: to die and rise in Christ. We die to the old, disordered self through the cross of Jesus, and rise up a new creation through the Resurrection of Christ. We are already pointing to the altar before we even sit down. We die to the disordered self of body, soul, and the sleeping spirit, to a resurrected spirit first, facilitated by the soul and housed in the body. We go from disorder to order, from chaos and frustration to peace. We go from being unhappy to being happy. We go from settling for the incomplete version of ourselves to becoming the real person God originally created us to be.

We also make the sign of the cross with fingers still wet with holy water. Now, I go to many Catholic churches all across America and around the world. In most of those churches we make the sign of the cross so quickly that many onlookers think we are swatting flies! It happens so fast that if you blink you'll miss it.

In the early Church they made the sign of the cross very intentionally, and with great meaning. They held their fingers in a specific way. They brought together their first and second fingers, and the thumb of their right hand. The remaining two fingers almost naturally fall against the palm of the hand. This has great significance.

The first two fingers and thumb symbolize the Trinity, and the remaining two fingers represent the hypostatic union of the divinity and humanity of Jesus in the Incarnation. So, the two central mysteries of the Orthodox and Catholic Christian faith are right there in your hand. Plus the wonderful reality of our participation in the cross and resurrection of Jesus are right there in the very first things we do with our body when we simply enter a Catholic church.

But it doesn't stop there. In the early Church they tended to touch their forehead, navel, right shoulder first, and then the left when making the sign of the cross. This is because Jesus sits at the right hand of the Father (Acts 2:33; Nicene Creed). Sometimes they touch the left side last because that side of Christ was pierced by the soldier's lance (Jn 19:34). This is still done in Eastern rite Catholic and Orthodox or other Eastern churches, but not in the Latin rite.

When did it change? It was the Germans! When the gospel was brought to the pagan Germans, they asked if the Germans wanted to become Christians. They said, "Ja!" They asked them if they wanted to make the sign of the cross, and they said, "Ja!" The Christians showed them how to do it, and mirroring the people standing before them, the Germans touched their left shoulder first. The missionaries said, "Nien, like this!" And the Germans mirrored them by touching their left shoulder again. They couldn't get them to do it right. So they figured at least they were Christians, and they were making the sign of the cross, so they let it go. Then it spread to the Spaniards and it was all over! Soon the entire Western Church was making the sign of the cross by touching the left shoulder first, and we've been doing it that way ever since.

Now, most of us are Latin Rite Catholics, so I don't recommend touching your right shoulder first. I wouldn't want you to look weird! (I often get a big chuckle from that as I stroke my long, gray, monastic beard.) But I do recommend holding your hand with the first two fingers and thumb touching, and to slow it down a bit. Make the sign of the cross intentionally and a bit more slowly. Cover your entire upper body, as a symbol of Jesus changing your whole life.

GENUFLECTION AND LIVING WORD

The next thing we do before we sit down is reverence the altar where the Eucharist is confected through the Word spoken by a priest over the bread and wine, or the tabernacle where the Eucharist is reserved. We bow profoundly to the altar—deep, slow, and from the waist. We genuflect to the Blessed Sacrament by kneeling briefly on the right knee before taking our place in the pew.

When we take folks to the symbolic Tomb of David, under the Upper Room, where the first Eucharist was celebrated in the Holy Land, there are many Jewish tabernacles on display where the scrolls were deposited. Catholics will inevitably say something like, "Oh, look! Just like us!" But they are getting it backward—our Catholic tabernacles are modeled on theirs. The difference is that we repose more than just the written words of God; we repose the living Word in the Blessed Sacrament in our tabernacles, the sacramental real presence of Jesus, who was the Son of God incarnate. In other words, Jesus is fully present there. It is not the written Word, but the living Word. This is a sacrament, a sacred mystery, the sacrament of sacraments.

Genuflecting was a gesture of reverence for royalty and major regional rulers. It is traceable to the ancient times with kings, queens, and emperors. It is said that Alexander the Great introduced it in the fourth century BC. It was picked up by Catholic Europe in the feudal system and applied to bishops and abbots, who were considered lords over the regions of their dioceses and abbeys. Since genuflecting was being applied to

Church leadership, it was considered most appropriate to apply it to Jesus, the king of kings, in the Blessed Sacrament. After being practiced anecdotally it became official in 1502 for the entire Latin Rite of the Catholic Church.

Now, here's the deal: All too often we have reduced our act of reverence to a perfunctory and quick head nod as we pass before the tabernacle. I have seen it not only with laity but also with clergy and consecrated religious brothers and sisters. It seems harmless enough, and it's better than nothing. But the last time I saw this gesture outside of the Church was during the televised debate between George W. Bush and Al Gore, when Gore kept walking into Bush's shot. After repeated "blockages" by the good vice president, Bush looked at Gore and briefly acknowledged his action with one quick nod of his head. It was hilarious, and it was certainly not a gesture of reverence!

Why is this important? We have a lot of folks leaving the Church to go to Buddhist and Taoist meditation centers to learn how to do "liturgy practice," in which a practitioner is "liberated" through the simple act of bowing or other liturgical gestures. Now, there is absolutely nothing wrong with learning about spiritual enlightenment through such liturgical actions. The Buddhists and Taoists are just doing what they do, and doing it very well. The question is: Why aren't we doing what we do very well? Why aren't we using the gestures and actions of our Liturgy so prayerfully and reverently that those who want enlightenment and liberation can't find it in their own local parish?

By merely walking into the church we should be entering into being born again in Christ. It is an experience of liberation and spiritual enlightenment. We dip our hands in holy water, make the sign of the cross, and reverently bow or genuflect. We come eager to die to the old, incomplete person who doesn't make us or those around us very happy, and to rise up a new person in Christ who is blessed and who blesses everyone we meet. We come eager for every action of our life to be one of liberation and spiritual enlightenment through the action of the Liturgy.

14: MUSIC

SINGING

The next thing we do in the Liturgy is sing. Well, maybe—we Catholics in North America are notorious for being truly awful singers! Other Christian denominations actually make fun of Catholic music as being "stuck in the '60s" and compositionally terrible, with even worse participation by the congregation. As a musician I must confess that I find this not a little embarrassing.

But the international Catholic Church is a singing Church. In Africa and Asia Catholics sing. Our community, the Brothers and Sisters of Charity, has had missions in Nicaragua and Honduras, and we know from personal experience that in Latin America they only know one volume: LOUD. VERY, VERY LOUD. They turn the PA system up as loud as it will go, and sing loudly when the Liturgy is prayed. When they pray the Liturgy in Latin America people on the outskirts of town can hear them singing. The Catholic Church is a singing Church, and only in North America, Western Europe, Australia, and New Zealand is it otherwise. There is a hilarious book called *Why Catholics Can't Sing*, which humorously explains the sociology of this tragic phenomenon, and I recommend it highly.

The liturgical worship of the ancient Church was a singing experience. St. John Chrysostom and St. Augustine described what they called "jubilation," in which the congregation sang out spontaneous vowel sounds or words like *alleluia* and *maranatha* so loudly that it could be heard throughout the city of their cathedral. They were doing what today we call "singing in the Spirit."

Patriarch (Bishop) St. John Chrysostom composed a Liturgy for the cathedral of Hagia Sophia, in Constantinople, to combat the Arian heresy and the phenomenon of people choosing to go to the Roman Circus instead of attending the Divine Liturgy. The Arians had taken to the streets with singing and processions to win the populace, and it was working. Patriarch John included processions and entrances that took the Liturgy to the streets with wonderful pageantry and glorious congregational singing. And it worked! They won the Arians back to Orthodoxy and brought the people from the Circus back to church.

We must do the same thing today. Right now our young people are leaving the Church in droves to experience the great music and singing in the megachurch down the street. Catholic Hispanics who come to North America are beginning to do the same thing as they encounter cold, lifeless worship in Catholic churches in North America. Honestly, most parish congregants mumble through the Liturgy and the music in it; we are seriously unengaged. The megachurches meet people where they are, and people respond, even though they really do not initially agree with the theology of the megachurch. Likewise, we have families being forced to choose sports over Church as young people are pressured by our secular humanist culture to either show up for practice and games that conflict with Church services or be cut from the team.

The way to compete with these religious and secular threats to the Church in North America is to do what we do and do it very, very well. A most important part of that is learning how to sing as a people. It is not all the responsibility of liturgical composers and musicians; it is also the responsibility of the congregation. We must do our part. We must begin to sing!

I visit churches all across America and around the world. I see the "premier" parishes with the best Liturgies we have to offer. Because I am a singer and don't want to draw attention to myself, I often sit midway back in the pews, and I sing at about half my volume in order to blend in. But even then, I drown people out for rows around me. I feel like I am singing a solo! Plus, the little ladies who sit up front (you know, the ones who "own" the pews) turn around and scowl at me as if to say, "How dare you praise God in God's house!"

But I know what you are thinking: You are doing everyone a favor by keeping silent. And if you were in the choir or a cantor I might agree with you. You see, sometimes we need to say to some folks, "Honey, this is not your gift. You need to become a lector, or an usher." But God wants everyone in the congregation to sing. It is an essential part of fulfilling our role. When we don't do so, we are falling way short of our responsibility in liturgical worship.

When I share this story in parishes everyone laughs knowingly. Yes, we know we sing terribly, and sometimes we even make pseudo spirituality out of bad singing. But we also know implicitly that it is not a good thing. It is something we have to change, especially if we want to keep our young people and growing Hispanic population Catholic.

God wants everyone to sing in his or her role in Liturgy. St. Augustine said, "Those who sing pray twice." The documents of the Church say that music is the art form best suited for assisting in liturgical prayer. The Church has always been a patron of music, and she is a singing Church internationally. It is only in North America and other modern Western cultures that we have neglected this great gift.

As I travel to parishes across North America it is apparent that the average age of our parishes is increasing. The number of young people who come to missions is small, and the older folks make up the majority of the congregation. While we have great turnouts for World Youth Day and youth gatherings, only fifteen percent of Catholic youth actually come to Mass on a regular basis. This is stunning, and not a little frightening for those who are planning for the life of a parish in our immediate future.

So one of the things you can do if you really want to keep the youth of our Church is to actually sing at Mass. Make it an event. Make it engaging. It's physical, folks! You must breathe in air and push it out with your diaphragm through your voice box, and make a joyful noise to the Lord. But it is your choice.

I have learned that churches get exactly what they want. Right now, if we do not change, most parish churches in North America will lose the majority of their youth in twenty years or so. There's an old saying that goes, "If you're not careful, you'll end up where you're headed!" Right now, if we do not change we will lose most of our youth and culture. One of the key ways we can change for the better is simply by singing. We don't have to sing all contemporary songs with electric bands (even though there is a place for that with youth Masses, as long as they are done reverently). We just have to sing the beautiful hymns and sacred songs fully. If we don't, I promise that our older congregants will die off until there are few people left in our pews. So sing! It is really a matter of life and death.

KYRIE: GROANING FOR NATIONAL SIN

Although it's important, fully engaged Liturgy is not all about singing or feeling good. It is also about deep, soul-searching repentance and prayer. So we almost immediately pause for the Penitential Act and Kyrie Eleison. It is the only remaining Greek in the Latin rite Liturgy. *Kyrie* comes from κυριοσ (*kyrios*) and means Lord. *Eleison* comes from ελεοσ (*eleos*) and means "mercy; deep compassion."

When I first became a Catholic we had an older priest who was a great church-building fund raiser. He was also a good man and wise pastor. But he was a terrible liturgist! He would lead the Kyrie like this: "Lordhavemercy, Lordhavemercy, Christhavemercy, Christhavemercy, Lordhavemercy, Lordhavemercy, let us pray." And I felt like saying, "Yes, Father, please let us pray!" It was rapid-fire Liturgy at its worst.

But the Penitential Act and Kyrie is a time to briefly pause and admit our deep and desperate need for God's mercy and forgiveness in our life. It is an extension of and leads back to the personal sacrament of penance, but we celebrate it communally, admitting sin and asking one another for prayer and help in overcoming sin through Christ and the body of Christ in the Church. As such it is communal, but is also deeply personal. It places the entire congregation and the celebrant on equal footing in Christ. We all sin, and we all need forgiveness and mutual assistance.

In our monastic Liturgy we encourage our members to look at one another during the confiteor, when we confess our sins to God and each other and ask for prayers of assistance from one another. It is remarkably liberating to give up the tendency to always want to be right in our conflicts with others. It is wonderful to just admit that we usually engage in such conflicts badly and are sometimes mistaken in our opinions about a situation, and especially about others' intentions. Such communal confession is indeed liberating.

It is also emotional and deeply moving. It is reported that in the Liturgy of the early Church the Kyrie was a time of deep repentance. In early Liturgies they prayed the Kyrie as part of litanies that called on the mercy of God and the prayers of the saints repeatedly. They especially prayed these Kyries during times of national and civic crisis and tragedy. Eastern liturgists tell us that in the cathedral in Constantinople they could hear people groaning and wailing during the Kyrie. It was emotional, personal, and intensely real.

The Eastern fathers admonish us not to let anyone tell us that we cannot weep at every Liturgy. When we truly realize how badly we need God's mercy we cannot help but weep a bit at Mass. This emotional reality is another area in which we can really be engaged during Liturgy. Rather than embarrassing us or putting other people off, it will actually draw those who are seeking reality in the Church. I am not talking about cheap emotionalism here, but rather an authentic engagement of emotions as a genuine human encounter with our merciful God during worship.

GLORIA: FORGIVENESS AND FLUID LITURGY

How many of us reading this book have sinned? I have too. How many have been forgiven? Yup, so have I. How many of you thought that it felt good? You bet! To be forgiven in Christ is glorious and exhilarating. That is why we pray the Gloria at this point in the Roman rite of the Liturgy.

We use the words of the angels at the birth of Jesus for the opening of the Gloria (Lk 2:14). But the remainder of the hymn is inspired by Scripture, yet not found explicitly in it. As a matter of fact the Gloria was called an "idiot's hymn," and was not included in the early Liturgy. Hilary of Poitiers (300–348 AD) and the Orthros, or what we in the West call Matins or the Office of Readings, are the earliest versions of it. But it was prayed popularly. It was not included in the Western Liturgy until the sixth century, with the Papal Mass of the Nativity. People loved it, so it slowly spread into the ordinary of the Roman rite in the West. Today it is included in every Mass except during Lent.

The Gloria is a response to the Incarnation. God will actually reach out to us in our sin so profoundly that he will take on flesh in his only begotten son, minister to us, and die on a cross for us. He gives his life for us personally. He personally rises for each of us, and for us as a united people. When we pray the Gloria we must respond personally.

The cool thing here is the awareness of development and healthy fluidity in the Liturgy. The Glory to God simply worked, and it raised folks to higher worship, so the Church eventually decided to include it in every ordinary Mass. It was a popular song of worship that rose from the people and led them in praise and worship of God.

But today we usually just mumble through the Glory to God. Especially since the third edition of *The New Roman Missal*, we fumble and mumble through it, just trying to get the words right. But that is not its purpose. It is a song of high praise and worship after being forgiven by God. It is prayed together in community. But it must be a personal response from each of us that causes a chorus to well up from the congregation like a Spirit-filled wave of worship and praise. If we pray the Glory to God in this way it will become something believable. It is not just a bunch of people mumbling through the Liturgy like sleepwalkers. It becomes something so engaged and spiritually powerful that it cannot help but attract any sincere seeker of God.

OPENING PRAYER

The opening prayer gathers up the entire opening of the Liturgy and points us to the next stage of our journey. That next stage is the Liturgy of the Word. The entire first stage has been using and gathering the senses, thoughts, and emotions of the human body to point us to the soul, or spiritual mind and reason. That will be represented in the Liturgy of the Word. So let's take the next step from the body to the soul!

16 : SOUL

SOUL

After the opening of the Liturgy using the body we move to the soul. This is actually laid out architecturally. We enter the church through the narthex, or gathering space, and sit in the nave, or seating space. Then we move into the sanctuary, where we find both the ambo, for the proclamation of the Scriptures, and the altar, for the celebration of the Eucharist. So with the soul we move to the ambo and the proclamation of the Scriptures.

In liturgical churches we have a special piece of furniture for the sacred Scriptures. It is not read haphazardly, or from just anywhere. It is read solemnly and intentionally. Scripture takes a most important place in the Liturgy. It is also to take a most important place in our lives.

Many people think that Catholicism is not a biblical Church, but that is not true. It has a special place in the sanctuary for proclamation, and is often enthroned as well. In Catholic Masses you cannot celebrate the Liturgy of the Eucharist without first having the Liturgy of the Word. It is the Word of God spoken through the appropriate minister that actually confects the Eucharist. Without the Word, you cannot have the Eucharist.

Plus, we Catholics hear a *lot* of Scripture during Liturgy. During the course of one year of daily readings and three years of Sunday readings, we hear a huge chunk of Scripture, and most of the four Gospels and New Testament. If we listen attentively to the proclamation of the Word in Scripture, it will slowly sink into our very being and shape the way we think. We may not always know chapter and verse, but we will find ourselves able to quote the essence of Scripture from memory. But we must listen attentively, and not just zone out during the proclamation of the Scripture during the Liturgy of the Word.

I have always been a bit amazed at how little of the Scripture is actually proclaimed during services at so-called "Bible churches." They have great expository preaching based on Scripture, and they refer to a lot of Scripture during preaching, but very little is actually proclaimed during their services. They know their Bibles very well, but we Catholics and liturgical Churches hear more Scripture than they do. The problem is that we do not always listen to the Scripture that is proclaimed.

St. Jerome gives us a timeless axiom: Ignorance of Scripture is ignorance of Christ. Say that again: Ignorance of Scripture is ignorance of Christ. Repeat this often. I remember the axiom we used in our Jesus movement days in the '60s: Seven days without Scripture makes one weak. One week without the Scriptures does, indeed, make one weak.

Scripture, especially the New Testament, is the earliest written record of apostolic teaching. But Jesus did not write a Bible. Rather, he was the Logos, the Word incarnate. He was spirit and soul in flesh and bones. And he didn't write a book. He gathered living, breathing disciples of spirit and soul, flesh and bone, from whom he chose leaders called "apostles." He gave them the power of the Spirit, who would lead them to all truth (Jn 16:13). Likewise, they gathered people, started churches, and appointed leaders to succeed them (Ti 1:5). They were an ongoing incarnation of the Logos in spirit and soul, flesh and bone.

It was only when they began to encounter problems in the churches that required their input that the apostles and their disciples began to write letters to address them. Plus, the rise of an affordable written medium allowed them to write the story of Jesus into Gospels. Many were written using the names of apostles. Some were authentic, and some were not. It was the authority of the Church under the apostolic leadership and the anointing of the Spirit that later compiled them into what we now call the New Testament.

To illustrate this dynamic in Catholic churches: We sit for the proclamation of the Old Testament and New Testament lessons, but we stand for the Gospels. This is because we believe that all Old Testament Scripture flows into the living Word of Jesus, and all New Testament Scripture flows out from Jesus. We are all about Jesus, not just the Scripture alone.

This is symbolized in some Eastern rite Catholic churches. Before they proclaim the Gospel, they come out into the congregation and gently place the book of the Gospels on the heads of those who have special needs. They so ardently believe that it is Jesus, not just words in a book, who heals with great power, they place the book with his life and words on the heads of the listeners in need, believing that he will bring healing just by attentively and prayerfully listening with faith.

I knew a guy at a Jesus festival back in the late '70s who said, "My life was a wreck until I came into a personal love relationship with the Bible." He was serious! I thought to myself, "There's something seriously wrong with that statement." I was not yet Catholic, nor did I know about patristics or anything like that. What I did know was that the Word we seek is the living, incarnate Word in Jesus, not mere Scripture alone. Scripture alone leads right back into the legalism Jesus sought to free us from. It simply doesn't work.

So the Scriptures are most important as the earliest written record of apostolic teaching regarding who Jesus was and what he did and said. But they are best read in the context of a Church that also has the inspiration of the Holy Spirit in our bishops and members.

The Catholic teaching is that Scripture cannot be properly understood outside the interpretation of the Church. Apostolic tradition and sacred Scripture are two currents in one greater stream of divine revelation. I also say that you need the three legs of Scripture, tradition, and magisterium in order for the stool of the Church to stand upright and balanced.

So we must pay attention when the Scriptures are proclaimed. They are most important. Scripture helps us to develop the "mind of Christ." (1 Cor 2:16) It is through the Scriptures and the teaching of the Church that our mind is focused on "whatever is true, whatever is honorable, whatever is just, whatever is pure, whatever is lovely, whatever is gracious, if there is any excellence and if there is anything worthy of praise, think about these things." (Phil 4:8) For whatever we think, we become. The proclamation of the Scriptures during the Liturgy of the Word helps us to find the very soul, or spiritual mind, of our worship. It helps us to find our soul.

THE HOMILY

Now it's time to have a bit of fun! At this point during my missions I ask the pastor to come up front with me and say,

"But the Liturgy of the Word doesn't end with the proclamation of the Scriptures. It also includes the homily!" Then I thank the pastor (whom I tend to pick on through the entire mission!) and ask him to sit down again.

Homilies are basically shorter sermons used in liturgical Churches. While Protestants are well known for engaging sermons, Catholics are known for rather boring homilies. As I've already mentioned, Catholics are notoriously weak in both music and preaching. But we have a history that is rich in both, and both are getting better today as well. This is especially true with preaching. Deacons, priests, and bishops are ordained for liturgical preaching. Lay preaching, teaching, and speaking are ordinarily exercised outside of formal Liturgies, but can be done within Liturgy extraordinarily.

I have to be honest in saying that I have heard some truly terrible preaching in Catholic churches. But I must also be honest as a motivational speaker that some of the worst talks I have ever heard have come out of my own mouth! Speakers are painfully aware when they dig themselves into a proverbial hole while speaking.

I encourage homilists to do more than just dispense doctrine; I encourage them to really share their faith. Faith has a way of eliciting faith within the hearts of the hearers. Like attracts like, and calls it forth. Great preachers don't all need to be Fulton Sheen or Billy Graham. They just need to share their faith in Jesus in an authentic way. But it must also be entertaining enough to hold the listener's attention. We preach not to entertain, but to minister. But if we really minister we will also entertain. The same is true of music. Most congregations are truly hungry for such preaching, and for music.

A good homily doesn't just depend on the preacher, however. It also depends on us. We must be good listeners if we want better homilies. Our ministers are trained to preach in seminary for four to eight years. They are finally ordained and get really excited to go out and preach the Good News of Jesus Christ. And whom do they get to preach to? Us! And you should see us. Some of us look truly terrible—bored to death!

We must become better listeners if we want better homilies. We must become active listeners and give visible feedback to the preacher. This is achieved primarily through the eyes. Look at the preacher! Give some affirmation when he says something that hits the mark of your soul. Otherwise he's preaching in the dark.

And you know how most Catholic congregations are. The homily begins and we start our internal stopwatch. We try to stay awake while the preacher drones on. We shuffle, stretch, and rub our faces. Then it starts: eight minutes; nine minutes. Then as we not-so-subtly break down and look at our watch we think, "nine and a half minutes!" But brothers and sisters, what you need to know is that from the front of the church the preacher can see *everything*. He sees everyone who looks at their watch, every nodding head, and every shuffle. And it can be terribly disheartening to a preacher who wants to really share his faith with his people.

I get to speak to congregations all across America. Most of the time folks have to be given permission and encouraged to have a good time at church. I try to interact with the people in the congregation and get folks to just laugh a bit. We live in often depressing times, and we need to be encouraged in church.

You can't imagine how disheartening it is to look out on a congregation of dead-faced folks. The body language of most congregations tells preachers that people who are unsupportive and bored to death are ignoring them. It is no mistake that Pope Francis is said to keep his homilies to ten minutes—because he knows that most people are bored at church.

Preaching is like landing a plane. Sometimes when we come in to make our point while preaching we look out on the runway of the congregation. And what do we see? Fog! The faces of the faithful look bored to death. So what does a preacher do when he finds fog on the runway? He goes around and tries again. A preacher will try to make a given point about three times before moving on to the next point. So if you want shorter homilies, give affirmation to your preachers! Nod your head in support. Let your eyes be light and attentive. Smile! Even give them an occasional amen. But not too loud, and not too often—they are Catholic, and you will frighten them!

PROFESSION OF FAITH

The Profession of Faith is the cap to the Liturgy of the Word with a few brief phrases and sentences that come from hundreds of years of development of doctrine in the early Church. When we proclaim our faith we are joining our voices, not just with each other's or with those around the world today but also with the saints all the way back to Jesus and the apostles. But we must make the profession personally. We say, "I believe," not just "We believe." No one can believe in Jesus for you, or make a profession of faith for you. It is a personal proclamation of our faith in Christ within the faith community of the Church. We do it together for mutual support. But ultimately we must make our profession of faith personally.

This is most important. We Catholics believe in entering into a personal love relationship with Jesus Christ as a united people. We believe in communion, or "common union." Non-Catholic Evangelical Christians often emphasize a "personal love relationship with Jesus Christ." That is great insofar as it goes. But it must go further to be authentic apostolic faith. It must be within the context of a gathering of disciples, a people of faith, or a church. And that church must be in the apostolic traditions that gave us the Gospels if we are to interpret those Gospels correctly in daily life. We take it one step further. We believe in a personal love relationship with Jesus in communion, or common union, with one another. That is the profession of the Catholic Christian faith.

PETITIONS AND INTERCESSIONS

Before we move to the Liturgy of the Eucharist we take some time to pray for each other and for those all around the world. We do this through petitions and intercessions. These are related but unique ways to pray for those in need. With petitions we pray for others from the outside in. But in intercession, we are willing to actually take the place of those in need in order for them to be healed. We do this through the intercession of Jesus Christ working in the Church as the body of Christ. Most of the time we are called to offer petitions for others. That is quite commendable. But on occasion we are called to actually intercede for others. That is extraordinary.

St. Paul speaks of the kind of love in which a person is willing to take the place of others when he writes about his Jewish kin: "For I could wish that I myself were accursed and separated from Christ for the sake of my brothers, my kin according to the flesh." (Rom 9:3) In other words, he would go to hell to save his Jewish kin if that were necessary. But it is not. Jesus has already borne the sin of all, Jew and Gentile, and it is his intercessory power that we now share in. That is a most intense prayer ministry, and it is given only to a few, in extraordinary times.

But in most Catholic churches I visit we just rattle off petitions and intercessions in rapid fire during Liturgy. Often folks can't even hear whom or what they are praying for, but we nonetheless mumble, "Lord, hear our prayer." Now, don't misunderstand me. God can and does answer such prayers if they are offered in faith. But I believe he would be even more responsive to prayers offered with heartfelt and active faith after we've listened attentively to whom and what we are actually praying for.

This is one of the gifts of megachurches. When they pray for others you can actually feel the presence of the Spirit in their prayers. The power of the Spirit is palpable in the gathering when they pray. There is absolutely no reason that we can't say, "Lord, hear our prayer," with heartfelt emotion and great faith.

So it's not complicated or mysterious. The next time we pray the petitions and intercessions let's really say, "Lord, hear our prayer!"

17: SPIRIT

SPIRIT

We now move from soul to spirit, from ambo to altar, from Word to sacrament. We move from the mind to the heart, from the knowable to that which can only be described as unknowable by the mind alone. We move from corporate meditation to contemplation.

We Catholics come to church not for the quality of the praise and worship or motivation of the preaching, but for the Eucharist. We don't come for the music minister or the pastor, but for Jesus. The music can be terrible, and the preaching can be boring, but Jesus always shows up. I often say that if the Liturgy were a movie or concert I wouldn't pay real money to see it. But if Jesus shows up, I can too! And Jesus always shows up. He is fully present in the Eucharist at every Mass.

Now, don't get me wrong. I believe we have a *lot* of work to do to increase the quality of our Liturgy. There is no doubt that we are losing people in droves simply because of the poor quality of our music and preaching. There have been times during Liturgy at premier parishes in large dioceses when I literally have to look at my feet and say, "You will not walk out. Jesus is showing up later ...And he always does!"" On the human level Catholic liturgical worship is often something to be endured rather than celebrated. This is not something to be proud of. There is an old saying that good Liturgy builds faith, and bad Liturgy destroys faith. We should never celebrate destroying other folks' faith because of our lazy and negligent celebration of the Liturgy.

But I will also tell you that there has never been a Mass where I have not greatly benefited spiritually because Jesus was right there for me. There has never been a homily where I have not heard something from Jesus for me as long as I actively listen with faith. And certainly there has never been a Mass where Jesus has not shown up and given his life sacramentally for me personally. Despite the work we must do to increase the quality of our Liturgies, it is always worth my while to show up and receive Jesus there. If Jesus shows up, so can I! And Jesus always shows up.

We Catholics have a wonderful gift to give the world. We have the real presence of Jesus in the Eucharist. It is a gift that other churches and communities often do not have or give fully. But we tend to make it most difficult for those who hunger and thirst for this wonderful gift.

It is like a restaurant that has the best food in town but does not have good service. The people come because they heard about the great food, but after waiting for hours, or getting lousy service, they go down the street to another place to eat because they get served, and served well. We Catholics might have the best sacramental food in town. But if we do not wait tables well, we shouldn't be surprised if a lot of people go down the street to another church where they are served very well. The other church or community might not have the full gift of the Eucharist, but they use what they have better than we do.

We should not blame them for "stealing our sheep." We really have no one to blame but ourselves.

I have a buddy who is an accomplished Christian musician, and he attends a well-known fellowship in Nashville. Many Christian contemporary musicians go there as well. The music is heavenly! The pastor, a Bible scholar, is a gifted teacher and preacher, so the preaching is stunning. And the people are welcoming and friendly. But my buddy says that after incredible music and preaching and some Spirit-filled prayer, he is really ready to go deeper into full communion with Jesus—and at that point they are blessed by the pastor and sent home. He says, "I feel like I went to a wonderful wedding, but didn't get to kiss the bride!"

We Catholics get to "kiss the bride." Music (body) and biblical preaching (soul) prepare us, but that is only in anticipation of the main event, the Eucharist. Everything that has come before is just preparation for the consummation of the wedding between Jesus and his bride. We are the bride. In the Eucharist we consummate our marriage with Jesus in the marriage supper of the lamb. It is deeply personal and communal. And it is powerful!

THE REAL PRESENCE OF JESUS

Let's move now to the Eucharist. This is most personal for me. Of course, when I became Catholic in 1978 I already believed in the real presence of Jesus in the Eucharist. But it has taken decades for that belief to sink in more fully from my head to my heart, from my soul to my spirit. Today, it is a reality that is simply beyond understanding and words, and it pervades my entire being. It fills me with awe and wonder at every Mass, and often reduces me to tears.

We Christians believe in the Incarnation of the Word, the eternally and only begotten Son of God, in Jesus. This mystical and practical reality was central to most of the theological development of the first five centuries of the early Church. But it can sometimes seem distant to modern Christians. It can be relegated to the intellect of the few who can actually grasp it. At best the Incarnation becomes an astounding phenomenon from ancient history in a faraway culture and land two thousand years ago.

But the Eucharist brings the stunning reality of the Incarnation into the here and now. The real presence of Jesus in the Eucharist brings him right into our midst at every Mass. He is no longer only a historical figure from long ago (wonderful as this is); he is also truly present and incarnate in the here and now at every Mass.

Let's think about this. God the Creator loves us enough to come from heavenly realms into our world out of indescribable love for us. And it is personal. His Incarnation is personal, and it is for each one of us personally. He comes from the realms of infinity and eternity into the created realm of limited space and time. And he does so out of love for each one of us personally. But in the Eucharist that stunning historical reality from two thousand years ago becomes fully present in the here and now.

In his letter to the Smyrnaeans St. Ignatius of Antioch wrote that the Incarnation of the Logos continues in the Eucharist. He was writing against the errors of the Docetists, who denied that Jesus was fully human and did not participate in the Eucharist. He says that this is because they denied his real presence in the Eucharist. Think about it. If you don't believe that Jesus is the Word made flesh, then it makes little sense to believe that the body and blood of Jesus Christ are fully present under the appearance of bread and wine. It is just a bit too "earthly." It assumes a belief in the Incarnation of the Logos in human flesh, and the presence of that Incarnation in the Eucharist.

It is also beyond human comprehension and words. All the theological arguments for or against the Incarnation fall silent in the simple presence of Jesus in the Eucharist. Remember the definition of *sacrament* as mystery that literally means "to shut the mouth." In the sacrament the time for words is over. It is pure and simple being. It is action. It is fact. But it is also mystical. It is a fact beyond facts. It is self-evident to those with faith, but invisible to those without it. It is the end of the argument for believers, and inarguable for nonbelievers. For those who believe, it is pure contemplation that is both corporate and intimately personal. For those who do not, it is fantasy, and something to be dismissed as nonsense.

At every Mass I am simply stunned that Jesus would show up for me personally. His love is right there beyond words. He simply *is* in the Eucharist. I am raised up in awe and wonder.

THE SACRIFICE OF CHRIST

But there is another theological aspect of the Mass that I accepted intellectually upon my conversion to Roman Catholicism that has taken decades for me to really grow into and understand from the heart. That is the sacrifice of the Mass. Though clearly witnessed by the early Church fathers, this has been a stumbling block even for some non-Catholics who accept the real presence of Jesus in the Eucharist. Let's take a closer look.

The sacrifice of Jesus for us is something all good Catholics and Eastern Christians accept theologically as part of the apostolic faith. Some even accept it on an emotional level. But the notion of sacrifice and atonement is something that we no longer relate to in religious culture. I mean, really, when is the last time you offered up some of your livestock on an altar at your local house of worship?

But most of us can relate to sacrifice on the level of love. We know what it is to sacrifice for a loved one. Some even know what it is to have someone sacrifice their life so that we might live.

I already used the analogy of the child who is playing ball in the yard by a busy street. But let's review it. A parent tells a child not to play ball in the street, because there is traffic and it is unsafe. But in the midst of play, the child chases a ball into the street, happily oblivious to the oncoming traffic. The parent sees the oncoming traffic, runs into the street, pushing the child out of harm's way, and gets hit and dies in the process. What parent among us would not do the same for our child? Most would even do so for any child. That is what Jesus did for us. He pushed us out of the harm's way of deadly sin, saving us and dying himself. That is how much God loves us. The good news is that Jesus is God, so he is raised from the dead by the Father in the power of the Spirit to prove his complete victory over sin and death.

This happened two thousand years ago on Calvary. Jesus shed his blood "once and for all." (Heb 7:27; 9:12) There is no need to repeat Calvary. The work of Jesus is sufficient for all time. There is no need for more bloodshed, because his sacrifice is sufficient. Likewise, there is no "new" new covenant. The book of Hebrews says, "Now where there is a will, the death of the testator must be established. For a will takes effect only at death; it has no force while the testator is alive. Thus not even the first covenant was inaugurated without blood." (Heb 9:16–18)

There is no *new* new covenant, so there is no need for Jesus to repeatedly shed his blood.

But the problem is that this once-and-for-all sacrifice often seems quite distant. It happened two thousand years ago in a far-off land and different culture to fulfill a religious ethos that we no longer even practice. It is all too easy for this glorious sacrifice for sins to fade away into an intellectual theological reality.

In Protestantism we often call this "positional theology." You probably have heard of or know the argument. Jesus takes our place so we don't have to suffer, and so on. It is a "substitutionary sacrifice," "propitiation," or "atonement." It is true. But our understanding and experience of it is often incomplete because it lacks our intimate knowledge of the cultural context. These are both Jewish and Greek legal ideas that are rooted in ancient sacrificial religion. We simply don't live in those times anymore. So for us it can all seem a bit cerebral and distant. But the shedding of blood is far from distant and cold. It is immediate and warm, like the blood that flowed from the veins of Christ himself. As Leviticus says, "The life is in the blood." (Lv 17:11) Again, it is personal—intimately personal!

The sacrifice of the Mass brings the sacrifice of Jesus on the cross for me personally right into the here and now at every Mass. It is no longer distant or ideologically theological. It is intimate, and personal, and right here and now.

Catholics believe that in the Mass the once-and-for-all blood sacrifice of Jesus Christ on the cross is sacramentally extended and repeated. It is brought into the here and the now. We call it the "unbloody" sacrifice. It is a memorial sacrifice, "in memory of" the sacrifice of Jesus (Lk 22:19), but it is not a mere symbol. It is personal and real. In this memorial Jesus is truly present, body and blood, and his sacrifice is being poured out for us today from two thousand years ago. It sacramentally and mystically spans the bridge of space and time.

How many of you saw the movie *Saving Private Ryan*? I found it quite moving. In the movie an army squad goes to pull Private Ryan out of combat because his brothers have just died in action, and the higher-ups in the U.S. Department of War will not leave a lone sibling in combat. The Tom Hanks character, the commanding officer, doesn't want to go back and get Ryan. All he wants to do is go home to his wife and family, and get on with his civilian life. But he obeys orders, and he goes. They find Ryan, and he doesn't want to leave his platoon, for he is a patriot. But he obeys. They start back, and begin to develop a relationship. The going is tough, but they continue on. They get to one particularly bloody fight and lose a couple of guys. Finally, even the Tom Hanks character is shot on a bridge. Ryan sees him, runs out onto the bridge, and sees that the commander is dying. The commander knows he is dying, so he reaches up, grabs Ryan by the collar, and says with his final breaths, "Earn it. Go and live a good life."

The scene fades to an aged Ryan kneeling before the commander's grave in France. He is weeping profusely. His wife, who is there with his family, approaches him and says, "What's the matter, dear?" He looks up through tears and manages to choke out, "Just tell me I've lived a good life." Wow. She assures him that he has, and points back to his children and grandchildren, who have made the trip with him. He is profoundly aware of what it means for someone to lay down their life so that he could live. Most military people who have been through something similar, or who even know what it is to lose a brother or sister in arms, understand this intimately, and are often reduced to tears when I tell this story at missions.

That's what Jesus did for us on Calvary, and what he does sacramentally at every Mass. That's how much Jesus loves us. It is personal. And it is real. At every Mass Jesus is personally and fully present, and gives his life as a sacrifice for us.

And here's the kicker: Jesus would have done all of this for each of us even if we were the only person ever to fully follow him. He would have come to earth, ministered everything in the Gospels, died on a cross, risen from the dead, ascended into heaven, and given the Holy Spirit. And he did it all for each of us personally. He knows us from the beginnings of eternity, and planned this "great rescue" because he loves us.

Do any of us ever feel a tad unloved? Yes, I do too. But let's not dare say that we are not loved, and loved personally and intimately. That would cheapen the sacrifice of Jesus for us, and would reduce the Mass to utter nonsense. But it is not nonsense. We are loved!

AN ALTAR CALL

At every Mass we have the opportunity to respond to the greatest sacramental altar call that can ever be given.

Many say that we Catholics don't do altar calls. Some revivalists think that we as a Church are dead on our feet, or what they call "God's frozen chosen." Some Catholics even look down their noses at the traditional Evangelical altar call as an exercise in religious emotionalism. But we have altar call at every Mass, and we are encouraged to enter fully into the radical call to follow Christ every time we pray the Liturgy and receive Communion.

Think about it. To receive Communion we must rise up; we must stand up and walk. The world is trying to tell us to stay seated and keep quiet. They want us to go along with the crowd of modern secular humanism. But we will not sit down and shut up! We will rise up and follow Jesus, even when it is contrary to the status quo of modern trends that slowly slip back into a new pagan barbarism.

We must also step out. We have to leave our comfort zone. We can get pretty complacent sitting in our pews at Mass—we tend to carve out our own space in the pew, and we feel secure, sometimes hiding there amid the crowd. This is an illustration of how we even create a comfort zone with religion. It is our own way of following Jesus, and we don't want anyone to challenge us to change. "Stay out of my space" is a common modern Western idea. "Don't bother me, Jesus—can't you see I am worshipping you?" But Jesus does bother us! He says that we must rise up and step out. We must leave the comfort zone we have so expertly created in our life.

Once we leave our comfort zone, we must come forward in order to receive Jesus in the Eucharist. We bring Jesus to those who are unable to come forward at Communion, and the rest of us must come forward to the altar. We must leave our safe place and follow Jesus in order to really receive him rightly in Communion. It can seem uncomfortable, but this initial discomfort ultimately brings comfort. The Spirit is called both "advocate" and "comforter" (Greek παρακλητοσ, *parakletos*) in different translations of Scripture (Jn 14:15–26; 15:26; 16:4–7). Jesus calls us to leave everything to follow him (Lk 14:26). But he also promises abundant life if we do (Jn 10:10).

What must we leave behind? Scripture tells us of three things: 1) possessions, 2) relationships, and 3) our self. In other words, everything.

First, we leave possessions, not because the created world is bad, but because we have used it badly. We are called to steward creation, not abuse it. Plus, possessions can posses us, and instead of using them we are abused by them. But once we let go of all of our possessions through the cross of Jesus, we can begin to use them the right way in the Resurrection of Christ.

Second, we must let go of all of our relationships. This isn't because relationships are bad—Jesus blessed marriage and family (Jn 2). We let go of relationships because we so often do them badly. We get stuck in negative patterns that continue to repeat unless we release them through the cross of Jesus, so a whole new way of relationship can be resurrected in Christ. Do we ever feel trapped in patterns of relationships that just don't work? Let's be honest—don't we often try to control others and end up controlled by and trapped in unhappy relationships? We think, "If I can just get everyone to think just like I do, then I will be happy." But even among like-minded folks in a common religion we have different opinions. Plus, it would just be boring! Sometimes we enable negative behavior in others and ourselves, instead of empowering each other in the wonderful things of Jesus Christ. Good relationships empower. But we must let them go before they can be raised up properly in Jesus Christ.

Last but not least, we must let go of our very self, our own identity, if we are to discover who we really are in Christ. Remember the section on spirit, soul, and body? We often get trapped in incomplete identities, and end up unfulfilled and unhappy. We place the body first, process it through the soul, and completely overlook the more primary spirit of who we are. When we let that incomplete self really die in Christ, then our complete self is raised up in Jesus. Then we can be truly happy. We can be blessed. We become the best version of ourselves in Christ.

As Evagrios said in one of his axioms, you must renounce all to gain everything. It is not about just giving everything up; it is about being set free to use everything—possessions, relationships, and our very self—in life-giving ways that bless us and everyone in our life. When we come forward to receive Jesus in the Eucharist we leave behind our old patterns of self, relationships, and use of the created world.

And we do this not out of religious law alone, but out of love. It's a good religious law to come to Mass on Sundays and holy days. But it only points us in the right direction. The goal is complete discipleship, reform, and renewal in Jesus Christ. The goal is to be "born again" every day in Jesus.

At every Mass Jesus makes an amazing journey of love to reach out to us personally. He comes from heaven to reach us right where we are here on earth. He is fully incarnate, and sacrifices himself for us out of love. And it is personal. It is no mere religious ritual or symbol; the presence and sacrifice of Jesus is real. And he comes to us fully in the Eucharist. He comes from heaven just for us at every Mass. He comes out of incredible love for each of us. It is personal and it is real.

So when we come forward to receive Jesus in the Eucharist at Mass we do so not merely out of law. We do so out of love. It's not only an obligation; it's a privilege. It's a good law to come to church on Sundays and holy days, but it's better to come any or every day out of love. We do so freely in response to him who came to us freely. He comes all the way from heaven. We only have to drive a few blocks and walk a few feet. It is a journey of love that changes our entire life in Christ.

So the next time you come forward to receive Jesus in the Eucharist, let it be an altar call. Let it be personal. Come forward for love. Give your life completely to him who first gives his life completely for you. As Scripture says, "We love because he first loved us." (1 Jn 4:19

THE PARKING LOT AND EVANGELIZATION

But that is only the beginning. We must now become him whom we have received. We become Christians, "like Christ." We become the body of Christ. We become his hands and feet. We look with his eyes and hear with his ears. We speak with his words.

This wonderful reality is tested almost right away. Where? In the parking lot! Most of my mission audiences understand this implicitly.

I often encourage parishes to slow their Liturgies down just a bit in order to really experience the richness of each part of the Mass. Pastors are very appreciative of my teaching on the Liturgy; they encourage me from the congregation as I speak. But sometimes when I ask that we slow the Liturgy down I see a clear look of panic on the pastor's face. Why? Because of the parking lot!

Some parishes where I present missions are huge. Some have as many as ten thousand or more families.. They have ten or more Masses every Saturday and Sunday. Some have grown so quickly that they have not completely kept up in their building projects, and one of the most painful symbols of this is the parking lot. The parking lots are works of art, where thousands of cars are orchestrated in and out of the church facility at precise times. Otherwise it becomes "mass" chaos!

So as I encourage congregations to slow down just a bit, pastors are in the back of the church motioning clearly, "Please, not that!" It is fairly hilarious. But I understand. We must balance the mystical and the practical in the local parish.

In all seriousness, the exalted mystery of the Mass is tested almost as soon as we leave church in the mundane realities of life. It could be in the parking lot or in the checkout line at Walmart or Target. Or it could be dealing with the family in the car. But it will come. The big things of our faith are tested in the little things of life. And it is usually there that we bring the most important evangelization. It is there that we preach. As the modern saying attributed to St. Francis goes, "Preach always, and if you must, use words." Actions speak louder than words. And without actions our words are empty.

We must become the Eucharist we receive. As the Incarnation is continued in the Eucharist, so it is continued in each one of us, and as a gathered community. It is a mystical wonder. But just as with Jesus, its authenticity is tested in the ordinary events of daily life.

CONCLUSION

So I pray that this little walk through the Liturgy will help you to never pray the Mass the same again. We hear reports after missions that this walk takes folks higher and deeper into the reality of Jesus in the Eucharist than they have been before. The narthex, nave, and the sanctuary, where we find the ambo and altar, come to life as unbelievable worship space where we journey body, soul, and spirit to and in Jesus Christ. They have attended Mass regularly for many years, or for most of their life, but they feel as if they have been somehow awakened to the truly universal and Catholic character of the Liturgy in a whole new way.

I am humbled by such reports. I am only sharing my own journey as a Catholic Christian. When I first became a Catholic I, of course, accepted the theology of the Mass, and it moved me deeply. But somehow it has taken more than thirty years for it to soak more deeply from my head to my heart, from my body to my soul, and from my soul to my spirit. I hope as you meditate on this walk, it will take you on a similar journey in Christ and the Church.

18: CONCLUSIONS

So that takes us through the Nothing Is Impossible mission I generally present at parishes all across North America. We are having a blast presenting this material, because we are presenting Jesus Christ and the Church to anyone who will listen. We are bringing a message of hope in a time when many, many people are discouraged and depressed. We are bringing the encouragement of faith, hope, and love in Christ and the Church. And people are responding. Catholics are ready to get excited about their faith again.

As we leave a parish I often say that I have given 110 percent through hard work in music and preaching that leaves me worn out. But if we get a parish to move "off the dime" of the status quo even two percent it is well worth it. And I am actually energized in the process. I am pushing sixty, but I feel twenty-five again! The Catholic Church in North America is facing a terrible crisis if we keep going the same direction. Remember the saying: "If you keep going in the same direction you'll end up right where you are headed." Something must change—and it *can* change. Nothing is impossible with God.

Neither extreme liberalism nor ultraconservatism is the answer. These things are only external. The real answer is a vibrant personal love relationship with Jesus Christ that brings us into loving communion with each other in the Church. This is an internal answer that brings life to all the externals of the

Church. Then we all move more to the moderate middle, where the left and right feet are needed to move us forward without tearing us apart, and we can confidently go forward in Christ to face any and every challenge from the world or the Church with the way, truth, and life that only Jesus can bring.

There are three major things I hope you will be inspired to do after reading this book: 1) Enter into a personal love relationship with Jesus Christ and begin sharing your stories and testimonies of faith with each other and the world, 2) foster that relationship through a disciplined and vibrant personal prayer life daily, and 3) join together in engaged and lively Liturgies that take us higher through great music and preaching, and deeper through the awesome real presence and sacrifice of love for us personally in the Eucharist, and give your life completely to Jesus at every Communion.

So remember, nothing is impossible with God. There are many things in the world that might seem impossible, but in Christ nothing can harm your essential being or steal your inner peace. The world might pass away, but Jesus remains the same yesterday, today, and forever. He is the still point in the constantly changing world. He is the "unmoved mover." Build a relationship with him and nothing will ever defeat you. If you find Jesus, you can truly be happy everywhere you are, even if it seems unhappy or tragic externally. Then, from that place of inner happiness, you will be able to solve problems in a way that brings joy to others.

There are really only two kinds of people in the world: those who are happy and successful, and those who are unhappy and unsuccessful. It has nothing to do with how much money you make or whether or not you will face tragedy. We all face tragedy, whether we are rich or poor. Rather, happiness and success depend on an interior reality of love, joy, and peace that is always with us. Religion and philosophy bring this gift in part, but only Jesus brings it fully. If we have a personal love relationship with Jesus we will know these gifts, and then we will rediscover full communion with one another in the Church through Christ.

The choice is now ours. It is yours. It is mine. And it is daily. What do we really want? That is a question I ask myself every day when I awake. It is the same question asked at monastic profession. It is also a question we must ask ourselves each and every day of our lives. What do you seek? You can have happiness or unhappiness, success or failure. You can end up where you are headed, or you can change directions and really discover that nothing is impossible with God!

God bless you.

To learn more about John Michael Talbot's
multi-facted ministry please visit:

www.JohnMichaelTalbot.com

To invite John Michael Talbot to minister
at your parish/event please visit:

www.JohnMichaelTalbot.com/Booking

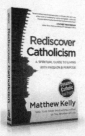

NOTES

THE
DYNAMIC CATHOLIC
INSTITUTE

[MISSION]

To re-energize the Catholic Church
in America by developing world-class
resources that inspire people to
rediscover the genius of Catholicism.

[VISION]

To be the innovative leader in the
New Evangelization helping Catholics
and their parishes become
the-best-version-of-themselves.

DynamicCatholic.com
Be Bold. Be Catholic.®

THE DYNAMIC CATHOLIC INSTITUTE
2200 ARBOR TECH DRIVE
HEBRON, KY 41048
PHONE: 859-980-7900
INFO@DYNAMICCATHOLIC.COM